REBEL ISSHINRYU

The 57 Challenges

Exploring Karate Myths, Madness & Mysteries

By Hayashi Tomio

Fresh Ideas & New Perspectives from
The Underground Temple

Wind School
Morristown, New Jersey

ISBN 978-0-9792697-5-2

Published by Wind School
16 Braidburn Way
Morristown, New Jersey 07960

Book Design by Kathleen Otis
Photography by Tom Maloney, Chris Goedecke,
Colin Goedecke

Printed in the United States of America

Cover image: Shifu Hayashi, 1992

TABLE OF CONTENTS

PART 1

*"There is only one way to avoid criticism.
Do nothing, say nothing, be nothing."*

Aristotle

PREFACE

The basis of this book is centered around twenty-five years of research into a dynamic, little spoken of, yet critical aspect of Okinawan karate-dō practice—its Esoteric Teachings or Internal principles. Clear and profound evidence exists and affirms that these principles, sometimes referred to as *Kiko* or *Chinkuchi* practices, were embedded into the essential kata of Okinawa. Isshinryu, as part of Okinawan martial legacy, is a recipient of these important principles and understandings.

My reference to Esoteric Teachings speaks primarily to those monastic martial practices recorded throughout the centuries and to those groups or independent teachers who preserved authentic and systematic accounts of the early martial traditions unknown or unavailable to the common martial art practitioner.

According to the late Buddhist Scholar, Nagaboshi Tomio:

> These teachings were mostly found within the members of three distinct groups; Ryukyuan independence movements, groups loyal to the descendants of the deposed Okinawan monarch, and Religious Orders. This latter recorded the history of their temples and teachings from China along with associated social and political circumstances of the time. Prior to the outbreak of WW2, members of these groups had begun to store or hide their manuscripts and ancient documentary records.

> All of the earliest complete forms of Karate proper practiced in Okinawa under various names had originally developed

from one main generic school known as the 'Shorin', of which different types were widespread in China. This name was the Okinawan translation of the Chinese name for the Shaolin Buddhist temple in Northern China. Shorin Kempo had been studied by certain sons of the upper class Okinawan families (*Anji*).

The Shorin Kempo tradition developed during the medieval period of Okinawan history was preserved by restricting it to a few and keeping it far from the common folk. At least two distinct streams of the Kempo tradition were preserved within Okinawa; that which belonged to the nobles and that created by the countryside peoples. These two lines of teaching followed very different evolutionary paths in Okinawa, seldom crossed. Almost all modern Karate schools were invented by village dwellers which contained only a very small portion of the full Shorin tradition. Most of the popular schools were in fact simply created by a very small group of ambitious individuals during the 1920's and 30's.

It is my observation that the Esoteric Teachings have only been partially revealed to the world martial community. Thus, the full face of the Martial Ways has not been fully witnessed by the Western culture's adoption of Okinawan karate beginning in the 1950's in the United States.

The biggest myth perpetuated today is that the karate currently presented is all that exists of these arts. The madness is that some martial authorities never exposed to the Esoteric Traditions perpetuate this idea, which creates a false ceiling of knowledge and dampens natural curiosity. In light of the growing evidence that we have profound, untapped, thousand-year wisdom inherent and embedded in our traditional forms, many mysteries behind kata's origins and potential remain to challenge us what these disciplines might still have to offer.

This work is an attempt to show how the vital cord of Esoteric Teachings entwines itself within Isshinryu. These teachings, however incredulous they might seem, can lead the curious and committed disciple to activating an extraordinary dimension of study.

This work is not intended as a how-to manual of Asian Esoteric Subtle Energy practices, though some technique is presented and simple tests offered to note the difference in the quality of performance. Historically, such transmissions were only and always imparted face-to-face, hands-on. Though modern communication technologies via video and written media are excellent at conveying fundamental concepts, they too often fail to reveal the actual, finer energetic realms that can validate the practices. These teachings were meant ultimately to be experienced directly, not just thought about. The subtle dimensions must be experienced with a knowledgeable teacher to affirm their validity. Also, this statement in no way implies that such information cannot be presented in a coherent, logical and sequential manner. It can. It is. And it has been. A master calligrapher once commented about the essence of Chi while drawing a circle on rice paper, 'Outside this circle you will not understand Chi. Once you are inside the circle, its nature will reveal itself to you.' This work points out that there is a circle. Its center is wide, inviting, rich with insight, and many martial artists currently stand outside of this circle.

Isshinryu karate, equipped with these new insights and tools, can be a forerunner in Western martial arts by advancing its own internal karate heritage and by widening the dialog about its future value to the world.

The more clarity modern sensei bring to their individual arts, the more options we can offer to our students and the greater the chance their value and meaning will continue to delight, to ground, to authenticate, and to provide practical, self-protective, therapeutic, and fitness guidelines to its worldwide disciples.

"Often we are most ignorant of the things closest at hand."
Nitszche

A NEW/OLD WAY REVEALS ITSELF

I'd like to share a story about your art, your martial path—*Isshinryu*. I doubt that you have heard this particular story before. My tale isn't necessarily better than the one you are tuned into. 'Better' is a relative term. This is simply a different story. You can make up your own mind about its value. It's your choice to take it or leave it. Everything you do is ultimately your choice.

In my opinion, deep changes have been unfolding within the world martial community since its arrival into the United States in the mid 1950's. New pathways of thought and action have been gradually opening. This new path is a result of long-term Western martial art influence, an ever-widening understanding of the scope of the martial arts coupled with advances in sport and exercise science in the workings of the Mind/body complex. Thanks to the Internet, some of the doors to Esoteric knowledge from Asia have become more accessible. This pathway has always existed in one form or another, but for various reasons, it became obscured during various cultural revolutions, recessions, and progressions, nearly invisible, and then, almost forgotten. I didn't create or invent the perspective I am going to share. I accidentally stumbled upon it, similar to the way you may have found this book or unearthed something unique about your art in your own search for answers. I wasn't looking for a new path in my martial studies. I didn't dream about it. It simply blindsided me one day with startling importance. That particular day was like any other day in my martial career. I entered the dojo to practice as I had done for decades. But from that day forward, now twenty-five years later, on top of an additional twenty-three years of traditional training, and after clearing the overgrowth, ambiguity and the obfuscations that can abound in these arts, I see this path with enough clarity to present it to you.

The tried and true masters of India, Okinawa, Korea and Japan have trekked into this frontier. This foreign terrain holds some of the quintessential answers to the big questions about our arts that we professionals strive to answer. Why are there eight Isshinryu kata? Why are kata performed with such precision? What is Ki? If it exists, how does it factor into daily practice? Where can decades of karate training lead us? In my opinion, the best martial practices represent some of the most venerable routes for negotiating everyday life.

However, this book is far from a mainstream thoroughfare. I am going to take you onto a hidden forest trail, well off the beaten martial highway. This secret trail is only ever walked by a select few. My story about my discovery of this hidden corridor is a personal invitation to enter it briefly with me here in this work, rather then give you a rehash of what has already been well-presented about Isshinryu elsewhere.

To be clear, my mention of a new/old route is in no way meant to demean, degrade, or condescend to any other path or methodology, known or yet to be known. I lay no claim that this path, or my story about it, is more relevant than the one you are walking, curious about, or listening to at present. I am aware there are many ways, alluring and exciting ways, into and through the martial arts. It doesn't matter to me if no one ever walks the path I describe other than the dedicated *yudansha* in my own organization. It also doesn't matter to me if any skeptics want to shutter the ideas I will present in disbelief. I too, was once skeptical of this very trail, so I clearly understand such a position.

If there are trekkers, particularly seasoned Isshinryu seniors within the Isshinryu culture who find themselves either unsatisfied with their present level of understanding or simply more curious about the potential of Isshinryu, I hope this book's perspective will light up your native curiosity, ignite your passion and invigorate your training.

I'm going to use some provocative writing to get my story moving. So *Agnostes emptor!* Reader Beware! You may get riled up with the contents of this book. That's my risk as a writer. My sincere intention is to fire you up, not burn you up. My goal is to prod you to the precipice of this new/old way so you too can peer into its vast potential.

SHALL WE DANCE?

What is the point of training, competing, fighting, defending, even living, if our actions are not truly meaningful, effective, and relevant to our personal lives? Seems like an obvious query doesn't it? There is little point to any serious undertaking if it isn't personal and conscious. With that idea in mind, the martial arts' many thousand-year history of being appropriated by individuals and groups from all walks of life to fit *their* needs doesn't mean it accurately fits your or my specific goals. In this sense, whenever we try to fit another's teachings into the relevancy of our own personal lives, we are all, at heart—rebels.

The martial arts have proven themselves a powerful tool for warding off the bad guys, if only in the imagination and confidence it instills toward one's future success in life. The martial arts have also proven effective for conquering or healing physical, mental, and spiritual imbalances. Martial training has awakened literally thousands of people to the core vitality and spirit of their lives. Yes, it imparts kick-ass technique to keep you safe, in shape, while offering stunning competitive outlets. But I've witnessed that many students actually stumble along the way to claiming their martial gold. The average U.S. martial student exits their art within two years. This is due, in part, to resistances they encounter moving thru their training; inappropriate tools, incorrect understanding, lack of proper guidance, scarcity of information, even misdirection on the part of well-intentioned sensei. Erroneous ideas about the nature of our personal realities often bias, not only the way we look at our arts, but the way in which entire generations have perceived them. We then unwittingly pass the art along wrapped in this bias. You've heard the term 'being your own worst enemy.' Admittedly, a fair amount of the resistance we face in both martial and daily life comes from our own ignorance, which leads to poor decisions, followed by worse outcomes.

Consider the sensei who lets us know that he performs, "the way he was taught." Do such sensei expect us to do the same blindly. Fellow trekkers, do not follow the way of no questioning, the way of no scrutiny. It is a dead end. If you want to claim your martial freedom, establish your martial *buyu*. Wake up! Take charge of your destiny. Be the co-creator of your own path with your teacher's guidance.

I have grabbed the richest of life experiences adventuring into the martial arts by meticulously following the mantras of the ancient masters, "Dig a small hole—Dig deep." After forty–eight years of blistering palms, slinging curiosity's pick into Okinawan karate soil, I hit martial pay dirt. I found both technical and spiritual treasures well beyond my expectations.

I did my time. I gave the conventional dojo ample sweat and blood. I dutifully tended the plot given to me by my various sensei for a solid, seven-day-a-week, decade of training: 'Wear your gi. Do what's told. Practice hard. Question little.' I found great practicality, efficient physical expression, and a good deal of personal satisfaction from ascending the Japanese *kyu/dan* belt ranking ladder. However, my days of following the leader are over. When I shifted my mental stance and began digging into the unconventional frontiers of the martial arts for two and a half more decades, I found a different set of answers, a foreign set of rules, far afield from the mainstream logic I had obediently swallowed (without really tasting) – offering me even greater allures—which I intend to share with you.

Sadly, I feel that some modern and mainstream martial teachings have stifled individual creativity and personal advance as much as

13

they have released it. Superficiality and egocentric dominance of information has become a normalizing and hollowing fad in the United States. Stale teachings blunt one's natural sensitivities for discovering new levels of meaning about our art. The sportification of martial arts in broad sectors of U.S. culture has sterilized and overly standardized a rich diversity of once highly-prized martial techniques and ideas. This sterile acculturation has compromised many of the art's higher ideals. Technical and spiritual ambiguities run rampant in U.S. dojos today. Isshinryu schools are not exempt from this carnage. The splintering of Isshinryu into followers of Kichiro, Ungi Uezu, James Advincula, Joe Jennings, Don Nagle, Harold Long, Alan Wheeler and many other frontrunners, has caused an each-to-his-own perceptual map of Isshinryu.

My discipline has been a long and steady foray into Okinawan karate, specifically Isshinryu. I have practiced the Isshin kata syllabus for nearly five decades and, although the style I now teach is an offshoot of Isshinryu, called Isshin Kempo, my heart and soul remains committed to the essence of the Isshin way. Before you cross off my training experience as 'not your style,' let me tell you why you might want to walk into this book with me. I have crossed a conceptual terrain regarding the most essential principles and techniques common to all martial arts styles and systems. There comes a point where any devoted student who practices enough with an open mind, will become privy to the primary framework, the overarching principles, upholding all the world's martial disciplines. This is a given outcome of active, alert and mindful training.

The word passion comes to mind when I think of my personal study and of those *Doka (Way student)* who, like myself, were bitten hard by the martial bug in the 1960's. I am as excited about my discipline today as when I started formal training at seventeen years old in 1968. In China, *ching* means passion. The Asian culture has a different context for the passions that our English language often fails to recognize. Those ideally, uncorrupted Asians don't see a separation of heart and mind. They don't view human nature as a series of compartments or pieces, as we do in Western culture. So when Americans *en masse* fell in love with the martial arts in the late 1960's to plunder its treasures, we mistakenly cut them up into bite-sized morsels to make it easier for our voracious intellects to

14

devour. Asking such an innocent question as whether the *'Shin'* in Isshinryu means 'mind' or 'heart' reveals a typical Western naiveté, foreign to our Asian martial forefathers. We over-engage our intellects with the idea that to get to the bottom of martial wisdom we must dissect it's essence into its smallest parts like the surgical delimbing of a laboratory rat. But by doing so we have played out a maddeningly obvious lack of perspective. It's an entrenched Western tendency that we just can't see well holistically. Just as areas of our medical profession advise the single pill cure to an undoubtedly complex body/mind synergy, we martial artists too often approach our arts from this same schismatic viewpoint. This mindset has obscured the story I am going to tell.

Under the guise of the 'one punch/one kill' hype, the martial ways is really begging us to let go the need to over-grasp the parts and instead, embrace the whole. Let the heart/mind live undivided, unagitated. True strength is found in an open, free, and spontaneously efficient synergy of self.

The Venerable Master Question

The most important question you can ever ask of your study of the Martial Ways, and ask frequently, undoubtedly the most important question for any true rebel is, "Why?"

Why was I being told that the martial arts were A, B and C and not to question the other missing letters? I even asked, "Why write this book?", only to self-respond that since I sought the answers on my own time with my own sweat, I gave myself the right to record them for my own informational legacy (and now yours, as it seems the right thing to do). I hope to go my grave asking 'why' because it's the preeminent, recurrent, life-altering question, particularly when the occasional golden egg of wisdom falls out of the sky and knocks my old-thinking head off as a result.

How do you get a new head in the martial arts? How do you learn to see what may be currently hidden from your view? How do you go from the naïve, blank-slated white belt to the hawk-eyed, white-eyebrow sage? The answer will never be found in the simple acquisition of a bunch of cool techniques. To truly grow you need a change of mind—a new head, replete with a new sense of eyes, ears, nose, and mouth. The Isshin Code states it correctly in advising us that *'the eyes and ears must see and hear in all directions.'* The real message here is to *wake up!* Wake up your senses. Start asking questions. Be an engaged, co-creator of your own discipline. There are a lot of training dimensions in the martial arts that remain untapped. Take responsibility for your quest.

This brief work hangs out my shingle 'Rebel at Work.' I hope to provide you with a catalyst for awakening—a new challenge. It's up to you to enter this book with your senses alert. If fortunate, you may find yourself with that new head.

REBEL AT WORK
ENTER AT YOUR OWN RISK
Practitioners *Beware!*

Why do anything the way anybody tells us? Are 'they' always right? What if 'they' haven't seen the bigger picture themselves? What if 'they' don't have the full focus or right agenda? What if 'they' don't have the right head—or worse, they lack the right heart? For example, what if 'their' agenda is to make more money from you or to assert their limiting perspective or ego control over you? If so, I say to hell with mentoring! I once interviewed an influential martial arts teacher on the East Coast who boasted that he could make his students do anything he wanted; squawk like a chicken, crawl on their bellies, dance like a bear—deplorable behavior for a person in his influential position. I am not talking about making young children do such in a creative class. These were *adults!* The ego needs of this sensei disgraced an otherwise venerable path. Could it be that we are practicing some things foolishly, blindly?

One day a gi-clad karate student waiting outside the training floor in a health club for his class to begin was approached by a member of the club who happened to be active in *Krav Maga*, the Israeli self-defense system. When he found out that my student was practicing Traditional Karate, replete with kata training, he shook his head in regret. He told my student, in a pitying tone, that he was being ripped off. "Kata is useless," he advised. He, on the other hand, was learning the *real* deal.

How stupid those old Okinawan masters must have been. If only Krav Maga had existed two hundred years ago, we'd be so much better off. How many people have adopted skewed perspectives like this? This practitioner of the Israeli system obviously knew very little of the reasons for the Asian creation of karate kata. But history is flush with misassumptions. It's not hard to see in this single example how easy it is to develop misperceptions about various martial arts. It's an enormously complex world out there. Wasn't the earth once believed to be flat by 99.95% of the living world?

How about the technical minutia in Isshinryu karate, whether the thumb should be on top of or alongside your fingers when you punch? Or how about those Isshinryu books that tell you Seisan stance is 'feet parallel, shoulder width apart,' yet, Isshinryu's founder, Tatsuo Shimabuku's performance on Youtube doesn't keep his back foot straight in Seisan dachi *most of the time*. Then what is the proper Seisan stance? Shimabuku also 'pops' his vertical punches upward likes he's hit an air bump at the end of his arm extension. Yet, we don't see many modern Isshinryu tournament performers exhibit this nuance in their Seisan kata. Most, if any, Isshinryu teachers even teach this to their students anymore. I suspect many Isshinryu teachers do not know why Shimabuku did this in the first place. Such technical oddities remain to be satisfactorily explained.

Have you gotten the deepest rationales for why punching, blocking or stepping should be done one way versus another? Many students are simply content to do it one way because that's the way Shimabuku or their sensei does it. Quite a few karate professionals have told me they practice a certain way with no further explanation than, "That's the way I was taught?" What happened to the natural scrutiny and curiosity to get to the bottom of things? How do you know you have been given the full, technical skinny on your art?

I began to ask myself these questions because I wasn't sure the answers I'd been given told the whole story. Some responses my various sensei had given me felt off base, only partially reasoned out. As a result, when the time was right, I rebelled. I exploded with better questions and sought more clarity and deeper answers.

That's when I made two major discoveries.

First, all the answers you seek will come to you if you put in the right effort to find them. The second discovery; we only got half the story about the technical diversity of the Isshinryu system. In fact, we may have gotten only half the story in all of Okinawan karate. When I realized this, my blood began to boil under the intensifying heat of my personal rebellion. I felt *gypped*.

I'm not suggesting a blind, manic rebellion in your dojo. You may be under the tutelage of a well-informed, talented teacher. Then again, you might not. I am not trying to incite a premature mutiny in your dojo or to undermine your training or your sensei. I am attempting to wake up karate-ka by broadening the dialog and dropping the ego agendas that have constructed false ceilings and divides between what we currently know and what remains to be known about the full face of the Martial Ways.

Caution, if you are a martial novice, you are not ready to rebel. A rebel is, by my definition, one who doesn't stop when stalled or stymied, but advances around or through resistance toward the core truth of one's practices. 'No resistance—no rebellion.' Without resistance there is nothing to rebel against.

Sadly, I've encountered too many modern day martial students whose rebel nature has fallen into a trance. They want everything handed to them, like babies. They want quick belt rewards without hard training or serious study. To this and I say, "Grow up!" There is no time for complacency in the world today. The enemy is emerging everywhere; apathy, ignorance, obesity, entitlement, rude language, incivility, irresponsible debt, greed, ambiguity, egocentricity, self-centeredness, entitlement, terrorism etc.. It's time to stir your pot with some challenges and to snap kick your thinking into new ballpark where you can contribute to the better part of this equation.

Don't get me wrong. I, and senior members of my organization, think Isshinryu is a highly effective close-quarter, fighting system. So did the U.S. Marine Corp at one point. But we also think the system has been under-interpreted, ready for a boost. Isshinryu evolved from, and is entitled to, a far vaster unclaimed technical legacy lying just beneath its current streamlined platform than it currently espouses. Isshinryu has additional layers to its kata ripe for peeling. Our own martial rebellion ripped Isshinryu's facade apart and found an even more dynamic system buried within.

Of course, there are the diehards who will argue that I am not doing Isshinryu. I don't care what the diehards think. I never undertook martial study for anyone else's pleasure or critique. I rebelled for myself and still continue to rebel for myself. The martial arts emerged out of what the Shotokan expert and author, Bruce Clayton, calls the *Crucible of Fire*—conflict and controversy. Martial arts train us for conflict, hot fiery, in your face, get on top or get burned, conflict. I'm well-prepared to both present and hold my ground. But what I am really looking for is more intelligent dialog, not a testosterone-charged mental fisticuff. If we have to fight for our art's survival let's make it a contest to raise our standards, because modern society is surely headed down a painfully wrong path, attested by anyone who has seen the decline in martial skills in the emerging young generation over the last twenty years.

Some will, no doubt, assert that what I've written is not what Isshinryu's founder Tatsuo Shimabuku taught, and therefore it is not Isshinryu proper? That is a debatable point. Let's peer outside of Shimabuku's sand box for a moment and ask, doesn't what you do with your toys matter as much as what toys you have? Where did Shimabuku get his martial tools? How did his predecessors use them? Just because Shimabuku played with his art one way doesn't mean it can't be played with another. With a set of wooden blocks I can make a boat. You might construct a plane or a tractor. I think Tatsuo Shimabuku took historically essential martial blocks and said, look at my beautiful toy train - the isshin cho choo! In Isshin Kempo we've crafted an isshin space lander. Right or wrong is always a matter of relevancy. Time will change the relevancy of every discipline. Martial art is no exception and Tatsuo Shimabku was well aware of this fact. If you happen to challenge the leading authorities and they don't like your tone of voice they will assuredly say, "You are wrong." But do they mean you are wrong to challenge their interpretation of the principles and techniques of Isshinryu, or wrong to challenge them? There's a world of difference in rebelling against a what versus a who. It's been my past experience that unbalanced who's try to get even.

This statement might shed some light on the kind of dojo you train in. My rebellion is about the what and the why of Isshinryu as a martial system, not the credibility or value of its individual messengers or passengers.

My rebellion also rails against what is becoming a sterilized mainstream presentation, not just of Isshinryu karate, (as I learned it, not necessarily as you learned it), and the system I've observed as others have learned it, but of the martial arts in general. Of course, as much as I praise the first generation seed bearers, I understand the obstacles that confronted them in the language barriers and cultural differences they had to surmount. Look at how little time they actually spent with their Asian masters before going out into the world to teach their arts. So it's always helpful to do some original, non-linear thinking anyway. Turn off the main road once in a while. Switch to four-wheel drive. Strap in. Get dirty. Get out of the stale, overly processed, white bread box, and smell some fresh martial air. Get ready for some close quarter combat with the current Isshinryu mind set.

We discovered, in the words of one student, "stellar" insights within this ryu. Rebel Isshinryu opens a hidden door to fresh observations and the untold/underground theories we found as we walked along what martial author, Nathan Johnson calls the Barefoot Zen trail. But be advised. Sometimes you have to wear shoes when walking across the sharp rocks of other's steadfast ideologies or you'll cut your feet to shreds and never cover any significant ground.

Old and the new Isshinryu are about to enter into an ideological ring. We might clobber your perspective. You might trounce ours. I'm banking on a synergy between the two. You'll never know the results unless you step into this ring.

En Guarde!

'Why' draws its sword on 'What is'

WHO AM I?

I have been a full time, career martial teacher of the Isshin path for forty-six years. I've conservatively taught over 50,000 classes to over 10,000 students since 1971, the year that Shimabuku retired from teaching. During the first twenty years of my career I taught 25-35 classes seven days a week, every week—without fail. I have many senior yudansha (black belts) holding ten to thirty plus years of experience.

Tatsuo Shimabuku taught his modified Shorinryu system, Isshinryu, from 1954-1971, approximately seventeen years. I've been practicing Isshinryu kata from 1971-2017, forty-seven years and counting, with no breaks in my teaching. I have taught martial arts to individuals from every walk of life and educational background, from elementary school to university level. I have taught Okinawan karate as a credit course for over thirty years at one East Coast University.

I recognize that the martial mountain is vast and complex. No one person holds all the answers or understands the infinite variations martial expression can take. I've had the unique fortune to make martial arts my entire adult life. In so doing, I have seen and experienced some truly amazing phenomenon. In 2009, late in my career I chose to become a Buddhist *Hoshi* (monk) and was invited into Esoteric martial traditions. This decision confirmed my deep appreciation for the wisdom inherent in a holistic, spiritually-oriented, martial art system whose goal is personal development and self-actualization.

To penetrate the wisdom of life takes time and considerable patience. Martial art, with the right mindset, offers anyone willing to look tremendous insight. My patience has been continually rewarded with a perspective that few students will ever experience, given the short time that most martial artists actually stay in their disciplines. As mystifying as some of the challenges I will put forth, I along with many others have directly experienced all that is presented in this work. I have never wavered in my passion to learn and to teach what I have learned. I stand firmly behind what I know.

The Teaching Experience

Certain phenomena characterize every teaching experience. A curriculum is formed and refined from experience then passed from teacher to student. Along the way these methods are reality-tested. In any ideal learning environment, methods and techniques that don't work well or are poorly presented get challenged or dumped. Poor martial teaching leads students to suffer an over-abundance of headaches and body aches. The educational level of an overall student body also shapes a martial curriculum. Uneducated students have trouble digesting high-level concepts. Also, the average physical body will undergo changes at a certain pace. Therefore, personal transformation is dependent upon the correct parceling and pacing of knowledge. So, if you enter a dojo unable to touch your toes by a margin of five inches, your body's ability to stretch those remaining five inches will depend upon you doing proper stretching technique, an appropriate amount of time spent stretching, and your body's physiological receptivity to flexibility. These features can provide a template for understanding how any martial technique or principle is learned and mastered. You need a specific and proper lesson, time to do the lesson consistently, and an understanding of how your body assimilates and responds to these physical lessons.

Does Isshinyu Need To Change?

From a civilian defense standpoint, no. The Isshinryu system is effective, direct and practical. Given that the average martial artist will train in the arts for less than two years, Isshinryu imparts all the necessary tools and tactics one would need to walk away with a viable self-protective competency.

Advanced Isshinryu however, presents a different story. Here, I would say that Isshinryu could progress by incorporating the Esoteric Teachings, which is part of Okinawan's traditional karate legacy anyway. Shimabuku was noted to have repeatedly remarked, *"All things in the universe will change."* It would be foolish to think he intended to exclude his own creation from this observation. This book outlines some of the ways Isshinryu could add to its advanced curriculum base.

In my opinion Isshinryu remains oversimplified at the advanced level at this present time in its evolution. At its birth, Isshinryu was a new and exciting undertaking for the Western world. Karate was an unexplored, exotic discipline. I understand why the perceptions about martial arts have changed today. Society has been dumbing down in the U.S. for decades. Our mad pursuit of superficial goals is pulling a lot of arts down. Fewer adults are entering into the Traditional arts. The large increase of children, twelve and under, whose physical life is being crowded out by digital delights now comprises the majority of martial students. These factors put a strain on passing the art of Isshinryu intact to future generations.

I must make a critical distinction about the focus of this book. I am not commenting on beginner level Isshinryu instruction. At this stage, things ought to be simple and direct as a necessary part of the learning process. Basic concepts should be sequentially fleshed out into broader, increasingly more complex ideas over an appropriate time period.

The oversimplification I refer to lies in the later years of training, for those ten-plus year Isshinryu students whose martial curriculum may not offer any further insights, but instead, fall back on a rehash of old material or introduce completely new disciplines. In many schools, advanced training is often a repeat of former knowledge.

Its maturing members are left with a scarcity of fresh ideas from within the system and thus ironically, begin to nitpick. It's sad to see advanced students flounder or trivialize their art when there is a huge mountain of information lying just outside of their reach.

Isshinryu is an outgrowth of a many thousand year martial legacy with dynamic ideas ripe for plucking. The forms that Chotoku Kyan and Choki Motobu taught Tatsuo Shimabuku contain exciting energy concepts and penetrating combat wisdom.

Part 2

THE 57 CHALLENGES

AND THE REBELLION TO RIGHT THEM

This section of the book takes a straightforward look at some of Isshinryu's mainstream philosophy, history, techniques, ideas and concepts. Common perspectives will be parceled into familiar, bite-size subjects; blocks/strikes/stances/kata etc., then challenged with some fresh perspectives in the hope of both stimulating your curiosity and adding new content potential into your training mix.

"When observation disagrees with theory,
go with observation."

Galileo

CHALLENGE 1

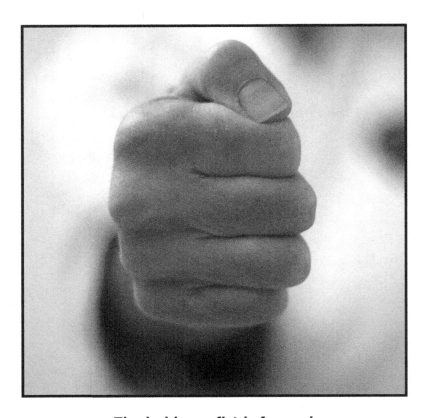

The isshinryu fist is formed

by placing the thumb

on top of the pointing finger.

REBELLION

This fist formation is considered a cornerstone of traditional Isshinryu practice. The punch is noteworthy for having the thumb on top of the fist as opposed to the more common, Western, and general karate fist arrangement of placing the thumb either on the middle knuckle of the index or ring finger. The reason cited by the Isshinryu community for the thumb-on-top position is its support of wrist strength during impact.

However, the reason for this Isshinryu fist position is not the only rationale for this thumb placement. To see what separates this fist from other mainstream fist formations let's look at the Esoteric Teachings regarding fist-making.

If the wrist is made stronger with the thumb on top of the pointing finger, why haven't ninety-five percent of the world's ballistic martial artists and Western boxers figured this out and placed their thumbs on the topside of their fists? Are they all that ignorant, asleep, or over-rigid in their thinking? Perhaps, Shimabuku was suggesting that there was not just one way to punch but many ways to punch.

My rebellion led to two conclusions; the vertical punch is not the sole Isshinryu punch. It may be the system's showcase fist strike, but it is *an* Isshinryu punch, one of several essential Isshinryu fist formations. Rebel Isshinryu recognizes three primary fist formations, each with a different thumb position for throwing effective strikes in the upper, middle and lower sections of the body.

Second, the given rationale about wrist support is not the essential explanation.

A properly placed thumb on top of the fist *only* supports a rising strike. This is crucial only when there is downward force exerted on the top of the wrist during impact. Such a force requires the thumb is pulled back and over toward the top of the hand to strengthen the wrist tendons to prevent damage to the wrist joint. Consider this; if U.S. Marines stationed on Okinawan during the 1950's, studying with Tatsuo Shimabuku, were taught a fist position that supported a rising punch, their fist would be fine only if fighting another of equal size. But if the Marine had to direct his strike downward to a shorter Okinawan, his fist would not be supported. The Okinawans would have had a much stronger strike aiming upward at a taller Marine then the reverse. This puts an interesting spin on Westerners training in Asia. Okinawan masters took the home court advantage because they knew something the Marines did not.

If you accept the exclusive thumb-on-top wrist strengthening rationale we want you to learn the whole story of this Okinawan fist formation. Don't take this statement personally. Maybe Shimabuku wasn't given the whole story of the fist. It's just a passing rebellious thought.

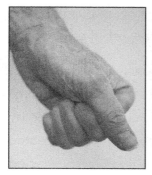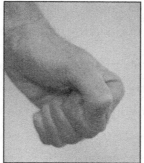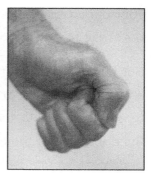

The thumb cocked back and toward the wrist has less to do with making the wrist stronger, which is supposedly evidenced by the protrusion of the two thumb tendons, Pollicis Brevis and Pollicis Longus.

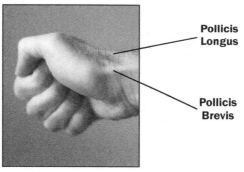

Pollicis Longus

Pollicis Brevis

This reasoning has merit, but it's not the sole truth. The two thumb tendons only reinforce the fist from a jarring blow to the top of the fist. A fist held at the waist chamber is always in a position several inches lower than one's own solar plexus, the basic training target. The fist must rise to this targeted height. This rising action also explains why Seisan stance is such a narrow posture. A stance does not need to be wide-legged if one is punching upward, because impact would meet the resistance of the ground through the puncher's legs. If you were punching parallel to your fist chamber you would need either a wider base to absorb the shock of your punch, or you would need to rotate your torso diagonally to the strike to better position your rear leg to absorb the shock.

But this rising punch fails to address other punching angles; down and in, parallel, left or right. A downward-directed punch requires tension in the pinky tendons of the wrist, which is accomplished by the tightening of the bottom two fingers. For a downward directed punch you would need to squeeze the bottom two fingers. Placing your thumb over the middle finger enables this extra tension.

TEST IT

Make an Isshinryu fist. Squeeze your last two fingers. Now move your thumb to the pointing finger then the ring finger. Notice how the last two fingers begin to grip tighter as the thumb moves toward the ring finger.

The rising Isshinryu fist formation reveals *Chinkuchi* or *Kiko* principles that offer a different explanation for the unique thumb-on-top formation. *Chinkuchi* is an old, Okinawan Hogen term that translates roughly as *muscle, sinew, energy control*. This practice is mostly lost or forgotten in modern Okinawan karate schools. Chinkuchi deals with the management of what, in Western culture, would be called Subtle Energy, the Subtle Energy Body or the Biofield. In Asian culture this intrinsic energy is referred to as *Ki* or *Chi*. In India, it is called *Prana*. The deeper rationale for the Isshinryu fist has to do with the thumb's location as a biomechanical gate controlling the flow of Ki in the arm meridians to give the muscles remarkable contractive striking power. In every forward directed punch, the primary punching muscle is the deltoid.

Chinkuchi is an essential, yet missing component of martial study. Knowledge of its principles holds the potential to dynamically launch Isshinryu karate into the next century. The full face of karate technique lies in understanding the internal functions of the Subtle Energies and how these energies can be cultivated then distributed throughout the body to instantly increase physical strength.

Each and every physical position you assume acts as a gating mechanism, in a small or large way, to control the flow of Ki, whether your action is a slight change in your fingers to big moves of your hips, to the raising of a single eyebrow, or to the flow of thoughts in your head. Isshinryu kata was built with this information imbedded in its core structure. According to James Advincula, Eiko Kaneshi, Tatsuo's right hand man, who started training in 1947, stated that he had studied karate from others including Shoshin Nagamine of Matsubayashi-ryu karate but no one had Chinkuchi like Tatsuo.

The Thumb's role in Punching Harder

Human finger dexterity gives us literally hundreds of ways of effecting Ki flow. The fist masters of Okinawa knew how to take advantage of this fact. First, just making any type of fist will immediately cause energy to concentrate in the upper limbs. This is part of the physiology of anger and corresponding physical power posturing. 'Anger' here refers to the body's motive power that supercharges our limbs in a primal way. Anger is reflected in certain facial expressions, specific tightening of the musculature, closing of the hands, widening of the eyes, etc. Anger is our most primal indicator of an internal power matrix.

Why do you think it is common to hold our fists above our waist in basic training? How many martial arts movies have you seen with rows upon rows of students sitting in the *kiba dachi* (Horse stance) shouting out while executing endless twisting lunge punches? The fist, chambered at their sides, captures energy in their torsos enhancing all their upper limb strikes.

The Chinese consider a closed fist a 'metal' action, one of five, distinct bio-currents based upon the Five Element Phases or Cycles. The Five Element Theory has been the bedrock of Chinese martial philosophy for several thousand years. In a nutshell, this theory provides a template for explaining the fundamental nature of all worldly interactions.

Ki is instantly concentrated and packed in the arms whenever a fist is made. An arm filled with Ki gives the deltoid, the primary punching muscle, explosive power. Think of Ki like the electrical charge stored in a battery—in this case, the battery is your deltoid. The object is to send as much Ki into the deltoid as possible. To direct energy correctly however, it is also necessary to prevent energy loss out of the deltoid, so a physical stopgap has to be selected. A river is not going to stop flowing unless you dam it. By placing the thumb on top of the index finger, Ki is both dammed and directed into the deltoid. The result is a more powerful punch.

The 'Five Element Phases' in the diagram on the adjacent page is a primary platform of study in the Esoteric Teachings. All martial technique can be assigned an Elemental value. When properly understood these orientations can be used for either practical/ martial purposes or for the generation of better health and vitality. The *Cycle of Creation* moves clockwise. The *Cycle of Destruction* follows the arrows inside the circle.

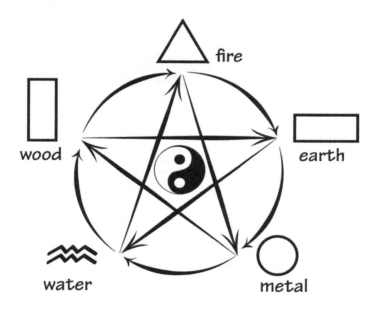

CHALLENGE 2

Isshinryu basics are *basic.*

REBELLION

This statement is only superficially true.

Digging into Shimabuku's fifteen upper body basics revealed a curious mystery to me, answered only when I held them to the Esoteric Principles. Since the Isshinryu basics under this light could be a book in itself, I will dissect just two of Shimabuku's original upper body techniques: Basic #1 and Basic #8.

Basic 1: Right Foot Forward, Right Hand Straight Punch

Why does this first upper body basic begin with the right foot forward? Why not start with a left foot forward, left vertical punch? If you think the answer is that you have to start somewhere, you are going to have to start back from the beginning yourself. In a typical drill of *kihon* (basics) you will not discover this technique's internal reasoning. Administering the appropriate test made the answer clear to me.

First, the details. As stated, the right foot forward vertical punch must be a rising punch and thrown directly over the lead right foot. The punch should not be directed parallel to the fist's chamber height or slightly inward toward the centerline of the opponent's body, assuming you are standing shoulder to shoulder with your target. Doing so goes against Kiko principles and will not allow maximum punching power. The right hand, starting in a forward waist chamber causes a barely perceptible clockwise rotation of the fist. This rotation moves Ki more efficiently through the punching arm. The fist can be aimed heart height at the stomach meridian. The stomach meridian runs down the center of the breast (consult an acupuncture chart). An impact to this channel

37

will disrupt the opponent's Yin energy and immediately weaken their body—even if the punch does not make contact!

This weakening effect will only be felt by a highly sensitive receptor. However, if you were to check the receiver's ability to withstand a strong push or arm twist, for example, immediately after performing the basic, you will see that he or she may have lost significant resistance.

What's most interesting is that this basic arm and fist configuration is only effective when thrown on the right side as a standalone technique. When drilling kihon it is often typical for a student to repeat the punch by alternating right, left, right, etc. Only when Basic #1 is done this way can both sides duplicate the configuration with no loss of power. But should the left punch be thrown by itself with no repeat on the opposite side, it will require the left fist be rotated slightly inward and palm down for maximum power.

Basic 8: Downward Block Followed By Five Punches

Throwing one punch is a basic. Throwing the same punch five times, alternating sides, is not just a clever way to get someone to punch more. Isshinryu Basic #8 is teaching the student about the importance of energetic rhythm, how Ki flows through the body to support maximum punching power. The correct pacing for this basic is; low block/punch, *slight pause*, punch/punch, *slight pause,* punch/punch.

Isshinryu's five-punch warm up is basic only in a strict understanding of the term. This cadence lesson and its rationale is too often overlooked by an unsuspecting and less perceptive martial public.

Try this test:

Ask a partner to assume a horse stance with their right foot back sideways to you. Next, execute Basic # 8 rapidly; block, punch, punch, punch, punch, punch. Try to push your partner out of their stance as soon as you finish. Repeat the experiment again. But this time throw the strike as follows; Low block/punch, *slight pause*, punch/punch, *slight pause*, punch/punch. Push your partner again. Many testers note that they can either push their partner out of the stance or that their push gained about 30-50% strength.

Note: Hidden variables can prevent the above results. A competent Kiko expert can guide you to maximum power. Newcomers to internal strength development are not energetically organized at the early stages of training.

CHALLENGE 3

The number of repetitions you perform

for any technique do not matter.

REBELLION

Most people will not catch this training subtlety.

In the Esoteric Traditions the number of repetitions matter along with the side you choose to start your bilateral training routine, that is, both limbs alternating.

In basic karate drills you are not going to see the full affects of your choice of the number of repetitions, which is usually set by the sensei, because there is often no strength test concluded afterward. Our Western orientation often sets the number of repetitions to the decimal system; 10, 20, etc, or one just stops the drill and moves on to other practices.

In Chi-Kung training it is quite common to perform a specific number of repetitions, often in multiples of three. The reason for this has to do with the bio-energetic switching mechanism of the body. As the brain distributes energy to accommodate the muscle's energy needs during alternating bilateral motions, it also seeks to maintain a homeostatic balance of Ki flow throughout the whole system. Bilateral movement initiates a type of binary code (1's and 0's) correlating to energy-in/energy-out actions. The goal is usually to end up with a systemic energy balance. Esoteric teachers note that some individuals need to let excessive energy out while others need to restore energy-depletive states to draw more energy in.

By paying careful attention to the number of repetitions you perform, you can maintain greater interior balance and store a more explosive contractive charge in your muscles. Sound, bio-energetic karate practice will increase your capacity to build more potential energy in your karate technique.

CHALLENGE 4

All Isshinryu sensei have the same

standard for black belt.

REBELLION

About fifteen years after its formal introduction into the United States in the mid-1950's, the Isshinryu system began to fragment. Today we have numerous organizations; the International Isshin-Ryu Karate Association, the Okinawa Isshinryu Karate Kobudo Association, The American Okinawan Karate Association, the Order of Isshin ryu and the American Isshinryu Organization, etc., each with their own unique vision and mission.

This fragmentation was primarily the result of instructional availability. Although politics and economics often plays some role in any organizational division, followers, in general, will naturally align with their organizational head instructors. Today, Isshinryu consists of various coalitions and independent instructors who practice the same system, but when examining the curriculums of these individual teachers, and/or organizations, although I see collective agreement on the kihon and kata, I also see a wide technical divergence amongst these groups at advanced training levels. This has led to the black belt standards, particularly the higher dan grades varying from teacher to teacher, organization to organization, and from culture to culture, depending upon which Isshinryu organization one is affiliated with.

There is nothing inherently wrong with varying standards for the black belt. The Isshinryu system as a whole could benefit greatly from a moderated forum in which the best insights and ideas from all the various senior teachers and their curriculum interpretations could be shared.

CHALLENGE 5

Tatsuo Shimabuku demonstrates tired,

old man kata in his captured U.S.

video presentation.

REBELLION

Shimabuku (1908-1975) was not quite a senior citizen at the time of his two primary U.S. video captures. He was fifty-six for his videotaping in Cleveland, Ohio in 1964, and fifty-eight at his video taping at Steve Armstrong's Dojo in Tacoma, Washington in 1966. Denigrating quips of "uninspiring" and "tired-looking" have been made about these performances. These statements were more likely made by individuals who do not recognize the ease of execution that comes from a lifetime of practicing karate. Shimabuku clearly internalized his art. In my opinion he demonstrates wise, soft-style, older man kata.

Observers unaware of the internal nature of the martial arts often lack the ability to detect or to accurately describe real talent buried beneath 'soft' performance, and thus are quick to cite the presentation as weak, lacking in power or presence. Those with first hand experience of Tatsuo Shimabuku's technique felt differently about his skills. He was fast, decisive, and aware of Esoteric principles. Shimabuku's videotaped performance is also to be called for what it was, a casual capture of the detail of Isshinryu kata for his advanced Western apprentices.

Probably the best-known example, by analogy, of Soft or Subtle technique that defied its obvious impression was Bruce Lee's exhibition of his infamous, one-inch punch. Prior to seeing Lee actually demonstrate this strike's incredible power, most martial artists would have guessed it to be far less dramatic.

I have two personal stories of unexpected martial power that left a strong impression upon me as a young martial artist. During my karate career I also took up the study of Tai Chi with a well known, East coast career teacher, Sidney Austin. One day, Sifu Austin chose me to demonstrate his Tai Chi push. I was standing about three feet away from a padded wall. Sifu Austin explained that he would push me at a rather unremarkable speed. The next thing, I'm lifted completely off the ground. My body slams hard against the wall and I nearly pass out. It defied my mind how much power he had generated with his 'slow' press.

The second story was related by one of the persons involved. During a social gathering two strangers discovered they were both professional martial art teachers. One was an advanced, Isshin Kempo teacher named Ott. The other was a professional Wing Chun Sifu. Typical of two enthusiasts, each felt the need to impress the other. The slightly older Wing Chun Sifu wanted to demonstrate his style's bottom knuckle punch on the other's chest. Sensei Ott agreed. The Wing Chun punch impressively jolted Ott backward several feet. Ott then demonstrated his palm heel press. He placed his fingertips on the man's chest and pressed his palm down into him. The Wing Chun Sifu was flung backward. He slammed into the wall behind him and fell to the ground, astonished at the extraordinary power of the move.

How many Isshinryu practitioners will move as smoothly as Tatsuo Shimabuku at the age of his video capture, or duplicate Bruce Lee's one inch punch, or Sensei Ott's effortless palm press? Shimabuku's ease of movement reveals more than the current interpretation or understanding of his kata. It's easy to sit on the sidelines and say that Shimabuku looks uninspiring compared to movie icons like Jackie Chan or Jet Li. But we cannot compare his performance against the bias of exaggerated, martial movie hype. The younger generation has seen so much dramatic movie footage that even exceptionally skilled, real-life, athletic martial performances can pale by comparison.

CHALLENGE 6

Isshinryu teachers clearly

understand why their system is

considered a Hard/Soft style.

REBELLION

A great deal of ambiguity surrounds the term Hard/Soft for Westerners in regard to Isshinryu. This is due to a lack of detailed explanation and agreement about what constitutes the concept of Hard and Soft.

In my work, *Internal Karate, Mind Matter and the Seven Gates of Power*, I wrote:

The traditional martial arts give us both an obvious, exoteric dimension and a not so obvious, esoteric nature. We label this dual nature broadly as the Hard and the Soft side of the Martial Ways. *Hard* refers to a martial arts external principles or its biomechanical nature. *Soft* refers to its inner or bioenergetic qualities and can include the movement of the mind.

The Conceptual Framework of Internal and External Martial Arts

In martial arts we use the term internal/soft and external/hard as an academic exercise to describe the complexities of a multi-layered mind/body system. For example, people often talk about the mind and body as if they were two separate but neighboring entities. However, if we were to take a scalpel and attempt to separate the mind from the body we would find that they are so tightly entwined that there is no blade fine enough to sever them.

This inseparability also exists between the concepts of Hard/Soft or Internal/External martial arts. Theses concepts are interrelated events. However, in describing the more extreme characteristics of martial practices we can glimpse aspects tending toward one side of the martial paradigm (the external) over another (the internal).

Why intellectualize this way? For one, such knowledge and aware-ness is helpful for nudging students out of training fixations that might prevent them from training in a too limited way. Offering students different ways to think about and to express their art encourages them to discover new tools.

Sometimes we hear mention of Internal versus external martial art, suggesting that a friction exists between them, as if these two terms represented enemy camps, i.e., if you are studying one, you must be denigrating the other. Internal and External concepts are not oppositional modalities of study even though some individu-als or martial communities might choose to present them as such. Internal practice is not better than external practice or vice versa. It's best to look at these two descriptors Hard/Soft as develop-mental possibilities, that is, I could take this road or that road to reach my destination. It doesn't matter which route you trek. It's helpful to know that you have options.

Consider, that any choice we make is drawn from a vast set of possibilities. For students of a more mental disposition, parsing perceptions into an internal/external format can be beneficial for stimulating the intellect to activate latent physical powers. Also, to become a truly dynamic teacher one must affirm and detail the path of experience if he or she is to activate this path in his disciples.

At what point does an external movement cross over into the in-ternal lane or vice versa? We need more precise dialog in dojos to help students answer this question.

Internal Martial Ways Practice

When applied to the martial arts, the word 'Internal' implies the interior workings of the body/mind complex. This complex contains a diverse physical, emotional, hormonal, and mental terrain with each facet possessing its own action tendency: The action tendencies of the mind include; thought, intention, will, desire, memory, imagination, intuition, and logic. The action tendencies of the body include neuronal, chemical, electrical, magnetic, glandular/hormonal, aural, photonic, and muscular motions. Internal can also mean hidden from view or hidden from mainstream or conventional thinking. From the Asian perspective, internal generally means the direct and conscious activation and manipulation of an intrinsic life force, an invisible vitalizing energy, the Asians call *Qi*. To activate our Qi first requires that we relax. Western science has been formulating a hypothesis about such a force as a confluence of many subtle energies working in synergy with one another. The New Practical Chinese English Dictionary lists eight basic definitions for Qi with an additional ninety-three definitions by various combinations. The eight are: Air, gas, vapor, atmosphere; Breath; Spirit character; Influence; Bearing, manner; Smell, odor; To be angry, or indignant; To provoke, to goad.

Because Qi has multiple definitions, both banal and sublime, it is easy to see how a westerner could miss its value in one's training, because the term, unfamiliar to most, also encompasses a wide variety of phenomenon, not all martial. In and of itself, the very notion of an invisible force seems illusive to most Westerners. However, the use of Qi in the martial arts has been embraced for centuries. 1st century Chinese are recorded practicing therapeutic movements utilizing gymnastic movements coupled with specific breathing patterns called *Daoyin* that would later be merged with Shaolin *Chuan Fa* techniques adding hidden leverage to oust assailants, to outscore competitors or, if extended into the spiritual realm, as practiced in monastic life, to overcome interior resistances and merge with the Infinite. We acknowledge this latter undertaking as the Enlightenment process.

Internal Martial Art, in its most encompassing definition, is the art of consciously activating, refining, and expressing subtle or fine layers of martial technique. These subtle dimensions include psychological, emotional, bio-energetic or Soft/Qi principles within a spiritual context of existence as part of karate's power matrix. Okinawan karate masters referred to the most tangible see and touch nature of karate's internal principles as *Kiko* (spirit/breath), or *chinkutsu* or *chinquchi* (sinew/bone/energy control). These terms were used to describe often-concealed aspects of heightened physical, and sometimes metaphysical, energy management practices and principles. In every martial art, regardless of how or why it was passed down, there is also an esoteric or inner rationale—always! I must restate here that there are advanced martial practitioners who do not attribute extra-ordinary powers to anything but a heightened body alignment/sensitivity or attunement.

External Martial Art

External karate is the expression of the overt, hard-wired or obvious gross physical nature of martial technique and principles. Where the Internal systems deal mostly with Qi management, External karate deals with what the Chinese term, *Li* or strength as applied through gross muscular tension. We refer to this basic tension model as an art's biomechanical nature, or in dojo vernacular, as its Hard features. External karate deals primarily with the actions of the musculoskeletal and nervous systems as they directly relate to and enhance the combative properties of speed, power, strength, endurance, balance, reactivity and flexibility in a Cartesian/Newtonian context. By this philosophical/scientific context I mean that our minds easily register and accept bodily actions that conform to the most obvious and commonly held expressions of the laws of physics regarding the use of physical power, through shifting weight and balance in the extension and retraction of the limbs. However, we rarely extend these same laws into alternate dimensions of movement. In a general sense, external karate training tends to place little or far less conscious emphasis upon refining the body's covert energy and communication systems. This is mostly due to the fact that the main populace doesn't know what they are! These subtle energy currents and inner events fall outside of the simplistic, conventional, linear cause and effect, kick/ punch model where 'hard' is all you need. As you will see, external karate relies more on a fixed, and sometimes rigid, understanding of the laws of physics. For example, most people would readily agree that a well-developed muscular person should naturally possess more power than a thin or seemingly underdeveloped physique. Yet, when it comes to demonstrations of internal power this is not always the case. It becomes more an issue of inner organization than of outward shape or appearance. Certainly, internal power can and is greatly aided by a healthy and toned physique.

By contrast, when properly organized and applied, one's internal forces can amplify gross physical power, because they draw from a confluence of emotional, psychological and spiritual wellsprings that are often restricted by our conditioned sense of physical laws. Your punches will possess more thrust, your torso will torque more intensely, your stances will become harder to uproot, your blocks will feel like iron rods and your mind will become unbendable and single-pointed.

Are Internal And External Arts Mutually Exclusive Practices?

No. You need a body to have energy and energy to have a body. To analogize, every coin has three sides: front, back, and rim. The rim, however thin, reveals the inseparability of the coin's two faces. Each side supports, links, and defines the other. This two-sided coinness may have been the preliminary understanding of early Asian philosophers who grasped the interdependent nature of all phenomena. This two-faces-on-one-coin concept led some Asian philosophers to seek a way to walk the rim of the two competing polarities of human nature such as good vs. evil, for example. The Buddhist kempo masters observed that all human actions posses a dual nature. Upon their reflections regarding the nature of self, they asked if it was possible to step off the 'Wheel of Suffering' (Samsara) brought on by dualistic thinking. For to flip one side 'up' was simultaneously to flip the other side 'down.' Good could oppose bad or good could complement bad depending upon one's perspective. Exclusively focusing on one coin side would conceal the other from the mind's eye (because this action was by one's own choosing, it was considered a form of ignorance by Buddhists). The coins hidden other side still existed, just not in the mind of the one-sided thinker. This three-sided coin analogy is also a truism regarding the underlying nature of martial technique. It is impossible to draw a precise line dividing Hard from Soft style technique. This has confused many regarding the nature of internal martial arts study.

Some masters don't see the need to discuss a term like Ki because under the right circumstances, when the body is working harmoniously, power just flows. I agree. Power flows when the proper physical and mental architecture or overall structure is achieved.

In my teaching opinion however, defining and categorizing various physical and mental organizations into layered types of techniques equips the intelligent student with a more fluid and conscious level of tactical execution, especially when diverse skill sets must be summoned into play.

Until the last quarter of the 19th century American karate-ka en masse expressed little interest or awareness in flipping their martial coin from its external benefits to its internal ones. Mainstream Americans initially perceived the art of karate solely for its effective but overt, self-protective and competitive benefits. When Americans first embraced the practical aspects of karate they were unaware that anything else existed beyond strong kicks and punches. This bias overlooked any internal training values, which lay buried under the topical ones. We did not embrace the spiritual implications or the refined internal infrastructure inherent in the Asian fighting arts because we simply couldn't see these aspects. It would take more than thirty years for this awakening to occur in the United States with the maturing of its homegrown teachers. In the meantime, generations of American sensei were blinded to the expansive internal nature of their arts.

CHALLENGE 7

According to one high-level teacher,

Isshinryu's 'internal' aspects

are *"no big deal."*

REBELLION

The three great martial arts of China, as well as some smaller Asian family systems and monastic styles, are built around internal principles and have had a healthy 17th-21st century run. During full contact matches in Asia, the internal martial artists of *Tai Chi, Hsing Yi,* and *Ba Gua* make impressive competitors. So someone is pulling rice paper over our eyes suggesting that a martial art's internal principles are, "no big deal."

The central reason the internal aspects of Isshinryu are considered no big deal is due to the fact that few, first generation Isshinryu professionals were introduced in depth to this secretive dimension of study. As a result, they never learned how to activate Esoteric Principles in their training. The Western mental perspective of what-you-see-is-what-you-get had us wholeheartedly embracing the biomechanics of the Asian fighting arts. What we could call the martial *bioenergetics* still remain a rare study for a select few.

In a personal interview with the late East Coast master, Frank Van Lenten (1935-2010), awarded a 10th dan by Shimabuku, Van Lenten, who studied directly with Tatsuo Shimabuku in his Agena Dojo in Okinawa, stated that Shimabuku never extensively taught Ki-cultivating techniques beyond the Sanchin kata.

It's impossible to make a big deal out of a subject never presented to you. But all things are possible if you are willing to open your mind to new ideas about your art. The internal aspects of Isshinryu give us an enormous new field of unexplored technical potential to tap into.

CHALLENGE 8

The crescent step is an

old world training method of executing

footwork in a semi-circular manner found

mostly in the kata.

It's actually much easier to just

step directly forward.

REBELLION

The shortest distance between two points is always going to be a straight line, today and one thousand years from today, not a roundabout, half-moon or crescent-shaped step. We don't crescent punch so why do we crescent step?

A core point throughout this work is that all martial disciplines possess two faces. One facade is the tangible, logical, see-and-touch, outer rationale or logic shell of a technique. The other face presents the inside story. I could use the word 'secret' here, but only loosely, in regards to knowledge not readily apparent or penetrable, not in the mainstream consciousness, not easily seen by the uninitiated, secreted away from our mental reach.

Some beginners introduced to the *Sanchin* or *Seisan Dachi* crescent stepping are baffled why one would choose to move in such an odd manner. Though many fighting styles adopt side and slip-stepping motions, few engage in half-moon or semi-circular stepping in actual bouts. Why not? The practical view by those who teach the crescent step point out that it can be used to either bisect an opponent's leg guard by cutting around and inside their lead leg to uproot their balance, or it is used to circle to the outside of an opponent's leg to set up for a takedown. These obvious rationales only reveal the technique's outer value. By contrast, the inner rationale reveals how the Subtle Energies are engaged to increase the crescent's overall effectiveness.

An informed internal master will point out the inside details of a technique. Chinkuchi, Kiko, or *Kokyu Ho* is the practice of the inner details. This is a different language from karate's mainstream vernacular. Of course, there are fighting systems carried through the ages that have the inner principles intuitively embedded into them. Some masters just flowed. It wasn't necessary for them to articulate what they felt. It was more important that they simply felt it. As stated earlier, this was one of the two historical pathways that lead to Chinkuchi's evolution. There are however, two distinct groups of internalists; those who have studied internal principles with conscious research and can articulate the internal mechanics of their art. These experts can give us a clear map for how to move through this unfamiliar terrain. Then there are those who sense the correct patterns but cannot explain why their movements are so powerful.

From the Chinkuchi perspective, crescent stepping is a Ki-generator. The action of the foot moving in an arc is something a straightforward step cannot accomplish. The crescent action activates all three Yin channels found on the inside of the stepping leg. Each limb, from an acupuncture standpoint, consists of three Yang channels (descending along the outside of the leg) and three Yin channels (ascending along the inside of the leg). The crescent stepping action activates all three channels. That is, the legs are either filled with rising or lowering Ki. Mechanically, a crescent step can be broken down into four paired, primary actions:

1. The foot moves forward or backward while passing the supporting leg
2. The foot moves toward or away from the supporting leg
3. The foot rises and falls, however slightly
4. The foot rotates clockwise or counter-clockwise. (This action is prominent in Sanchin dachi stepping).

Chinkuchi crescent stepping is a more specific action than just gliding the foot in an arc over the ground. It involves a precise movement of the upper thigh and foreleg, and the arc must cross the body's mid-line (spine), skim low to the ground, with weight forward on the balls of the feet, and the feet must assume a particular proportionality in length and width to maintain an open flow of energy in the foot's Bubbling Springs acupressure point. The crescent action of the left and right foot are also not identical motions from a Subtle Energy standpoint. The left foot forward crescent is considered a Yin action, the right forward step, Yang.

There are additional bioenergetic fundamentals to crescent stepping that require greater explanation than this book affords that are seemingly unknown or unavailable to the Isshinryu community at this time. Few modern Isshinryu experts possess comprehensive knowledge of the internal mechanisms of the ryu to fully activate its Chinkuchi principles.

In this and future works our organization will provide a catalyst for an emerging Internal Isshinryu to benefit the international Isshinryu community and those interested in this exciting, though currently mysterious, study.

CHALLENGE 9

The Horse and *Seiuchin* stances are
roughly the same postures. It only matters
that you stand wide-legged when
greater stability is needed.

REBELLION

At a quick glance these two stances appear roughly similar. However, the *Kiba dachi* (Horse stance) and the *Seiuchin* dachi (pulling/controlling stance) or what is also called the *Shiko* dachi (rock solid stance) are two very different postures. Each represents a distinct, internal energy formula. Because mainstream karate practitioners never got the whole body energy fundamentals of these two stances their critical differences often get overlooked.

There is some plausibility to the fact that those who cannot assume a proper Horse stance would find the Seiuchin dachi the next logical posture, as turning the feet outward relieves any strain on the ankles and knees. But this is not the intended rational why one stance was chosen over another. Each posture creates a different energy flow in the leg meridians, which in turn affects strength in either the lats, triceps, or deltoid muscles.

Putting aside the relief from any anatomical restrictions that keeps a student's feet turned in or out to avoid unnecessary strain, I will list the biomechanical differences that separate these two postures as a prerequisite for their internal study.

Horse Stance (Kiba Dachi) Fundamentals:

Feet are a prescribed 1 1/2 shoulder width apart. Chin in, head straight but not stiff. Knees out. Pelvis tucked forward. Back straight. Concentration is held on the *Hara* (belly).

Seiuchin or Shiko Dachi Stance Fundamentals:

Same width as the Horse Stance. However, the chin is extended slightly forward. The pelvis is tilted back, which causes the upper torso to tilt slightly forward. Knees out.

Chinkuchi practitioners note the formulaic width to all stances has a margin of error of two to three inches before a polarity change weakens the motion.

Here are some further observations on the Horse stance from my book, *The Soul Polisher's Apprentice*:

The Horse stance is the foundational posture for many of the world's fighting styles. All martial stances originated from the Horse posture. The oldest placement of the feet according to one Qi Gong master is forward with the knees bowed so the body's weight does not degrade the knee joints. In martial arts you need a strong foundation. Horse stance provides tremendous leg development. In addition, there is a particular array of blood vessels in the calf the Chinese call the (Lower Hearts). The Horse stance strengthens the calf muscles that enhance their circulation. Unfortunately, some modern systems lump the Horse stance into a category of any low-legged, leg-parallel posture with or without the feet at various angles.

The southern-style Kung Fu adept and herbologist, Jake Jacobowski, with over forty years of martial experience, points out that two-thirds of our life force comes from our breath. One-third comes from the ground up through the feet at a point called the Bubbling Springs.

'The Horse stance, affords the greatest draw of ki. This posture, in particular, allows the feet to compress and the Bubbling Springs to open. Because the Bubbling Springs lie along the Kidney channel this action is sometimes called Kidney Breathing.

Stance training lays the first foundation for unity of mind, body, and spirit. That foundation begins with concentration and relaxation. *'All movement comes from stillness,'* as written in the Tao De Ching. The Horse stance not only provides that stillness but fills the subtle energy reservoir.

The value of Horse stance is lost to many schools. Some modern instructors make little or no distinction how their feet are placed apart. Turning the feet outward alters the stance into an entirely different energy flow than keeping them straight. Ki flow is altered with slight angles of the feet. These shifts were deemed significant enough that the old masters packed their kata with this knowledge. Seiuchin kata was designed for optimum execution of its waza, with the feet outward in the Seiuchin stance, not in the parallel feet of the Horse stance.

A novice will not realize the value of these distinctions at a basic training level. You must remember that karate strikes, joint locks, takedowns, particularly kicking skills, were novel exports from Asia to a 1960's western boxing culture. We took these ideas at their practical, face value. The majority of the martial art community hasn't grasped the tremendous Internal Energy potential behind their arts.

Also, all static and dynamic physical posturing is a form of acupressure. Standing in Horse twenty minutes a day will cause detectable changes. Support musculature strengthens. If your legs are unequally weighted, your spine will be affected. If your spine is affected, the flow of nerve energy traveling the spinal cord will be effected. The more extreme the posture, the more dramatic the ki flow in the meridians. Imbalance in the posture will cause imbalances in the musculature, body organs, and mind.

Early martial explorers surmised that certain strikes, locks, parries, and so on were more powerful when executed from a particular stance. Kata teaches those strength configurations. Still, many martial artists bog down from the habitual repetition of adequate level technique. Adequate techniques work because one's opponents are not any more knowledgeable about neutralizing them. Mediocrity in the martial community has caused a stagnation of advanced ideas about internal practice.

CHALLENGE 10

A kata's formal salutation is a fixed

ritual and generally the same for each

Form. It doesn't matter if you bow or not.

The salutation has little relevance

to kata bunkai.

REBELLION

Not true.

Martial salutations are a mixture of military, monastic, and village customs. Even the modern military salute of most countries reveals an esoteric, internal nature. At the height of martial knowledge in Asia, various salutations were used to charge or activate the opening moves of a fighting pattern. In addition, some ritual openings were hidden *bunkai* themselves.

One of Okinawa's most highly respected Shorin masters, Shoshin Nagamine (1907-1997), a virtual treasure of Okinawan karate knowledge during his lifetime, illustrated, in his book, *The Essence of Okinawan Karate*, different salutations for initiating his Shorin kata. Nagamine never mentions the reason for the varied salutational actions. He simply notes what they are. When I saw these unique positions, I knew, unmistakably, the reason for the slight postural adjustments were meant to activate Kiko principles for the kata movements to follow.

It was also Nagamine who stated, *"If you are not doing kata, you are not doing karate."* This master's comment says it all. Okinawan kata carry the true depth of both principles and techniques in its formal patterns. Your job is to unlock and master them.

CHALLENGE 11

It doesn't matter if you train in a T-shirt
and sweats, leisure suit, naked, a natural
fabric, or a cotton/poly blended karate
uniform. It is still the same workout.
The same sweat rolls off your body.

REBELLION

Your training wear absolutely matters.

A traditional karate *gi* offers you the practical value of allowing forceful tugs, grips, and free, unrestricted movement of the body. Rarely known is that the gi's design facilitates the natural flow of Ki around the body, evidenced by the jacket wrapping from left to right around the waist.

Training gear or apparel that fits too tightly acts like a contracted muscle on the Energy Body. Tight muscle shuts off Ki flow. Therefore, both the karate pants and obi should be worn loosely around the waist. If either is wrapped too tightly the resulting tension will inhibit the concentration of Ki in the *dantien* where the Ki pools, which will cause a drop in overall physical strength.

Also, the belt tabs of the obi should hang to the inside of the thighs. Depending upon the thickness of the obi, the tab length should be no shorter then six inches to ensure the tabs hang downward inside the thighs and not stretch sideways across the waistline.

Despite their undeniable cost effectiveness, synthetic materials such as cotton-poly blended karate uniforms inhibit Ki flow. The energy fields produced by synthetic clothing cause certain meridian channels to constrict, reducing overall strength. Ki is *subtle* energy. It is particularly sensitive to shifts in the surrounding radiating fields given off by all objects. These fields include clothing and the training gear we wear as well as color, cut, shape, and pressures exerted. Our energy field reacts instantly to the radiating energy fields of both animate and inanimate objects.

Technology is challenging the internal equation of karate practice with the invention of ever-new training products. Martial footwear is a case in point. Logically, footwear offers us better hygiene and foot protection. However, shoes and socks of varying materials, shapes, pressures, and colors alter the body's subtle energy flow. Wearing Nike's one day, New Balance another, or white cotton socks one day and gray cotton-polys the next, also alters Ki's circulation through the legs. Bare feet offer us a constant training variable. If everyone practiced in the same shoes and socks this would not be a problem. Consistency in training variables enables the internal practitioners to develop critical sensitivities.

CHALLENGE 12

When you *kiai*, just shout loudly.

A kiai at certain points in the kata startles

the opponent.

REBELLION

"Just shout" is a gross oversimplification of the *kiai*.

This advice is akin to saying "just punch" to a martial novice or "just strum" when learning to play a guitar, without any further instructions.

An Isshinryu nidan once asked me why I didn't direct my student's to kiai at the required spots in Seisan kata. I returned his question asking, "Why do you kiai at those spots? He explained how the shout startles the opponent. I replied, "If that is true, why not kiai on every move?" He was stumped. His teacher, whose response I predicted, remarked, "Because that is the way I was taught."

This answer is not good enough for a true rebel. So what is a kiai? Why must it fall at certain moves in a kata?

Mainstream Isshinryu can benefit from a clearer definition between a true kiai and a *kakegoe*. A *kakegoe* is a simple shout. A Kiai is also a shout, but its older meaning is to meet (*ai*) each other's spiritual energy (*ki*). According to Aikibudo expert Arakawa Tomio, "The Kiai must be legitimately presented as a particular shout with specialized breathing techniques or no shout at all with specialized breathing techniques called *Kokyu* or *Kokyu-Ho*."

Vocal intonations along the tonal scale produce energy frequencies that prompt meridian flow to constrict or dilate causing a strengthening or weakening of specific musculature in your opponent's body. Simply put, both audible and silent shouts (the intent to shout without any audible sound being made) in the upper octave will strengthen rising limb motions. Strikes in the lower

75

octaves will strengthen pulling/drawing motions.

All our actions are activated by our intention. Audible and inaudible or silent shouts trigger an internal template in the body/mind complex that alters meridian flow. These activated meridians in turn energize specific muscles.

Shouts that occur at different points in an Isshinryu kata sequence are done with various pitches to switch on certain channels.

Historical reasons for the kiai:

• The shout jars students out of an automatic pilot performance, similar to getting hit by the Buddhist *Kyosaku* (bamboo meditation stick).

• A kiai served as a tactical, team-coordinated, command that can be heard over the din of a mass attack (to attack, retreat or take hostages).

• The kiai stimulates certain acupoints to increase power to the body and/or decrease the strength of the adversary.

• The kiai is used to distract or draw the attention of an opponent to or away from one's real intention.

• The kiai is used to disrupt a person's nervous system. The 'fight or flight' response activates the sympathetic nervous system sending the body into high gear. Initially, most people are momentarily disoriented when a loud, unexpected shout occurs, creating an element of advantageous surprise.

CHALLENGE 13

Kata should be done equally on both

sides of the body. It does not matter which

side you practice your kata on.

Both are effective.

REBELLION

If kata is to be performed as a mirror image to develop equal side effectiveness, why haven't all the old school sensei made sure that their students performed kata on both sides? Instead, we see an historical emphasis to not only perform kata on one side, but to initiate basic technique starting with one side first.

OKinawan karate katas were designed to be practiced on one side for a reason. An example of this reasoning can be found in the Seisan kata's step/middle-block/punch/punch/kick/punch sequence. Okinawan masters knew that too many choices during the heat of a conflict made for poor execution, which could easily lead to failure. Their idea—simplify the physical exchange. Defensively, they taught that a left middle block will effectively counter both a right or left arm attack. Using the left side to parry is in alignment with Kiko principles because the left parry is a Yin (energy-in) action (if done properly). Therefore, it was the preferred choice for blocking. They did not want to muddle a defender's mind by having to pair right attacks with left blocks, and left attacks with right blocks. Strikes are thrown in fractions of a second. Too much thinking increases the probability of a mistake. Maintaining the left side as the blocking side resolved which arm to defend with and simplified the defensive strategy.

In the case where you see a technique performed on both sides within a single kata, the originators were conveying that such a movement sequence was important enough to warrant being repeated as a mirror image but—these mirror actions would often display slight technical nuances.

Using the principles of internal energy distribution, you can adapt any kata to its mirror image and maintain a high degree of effectiveness. What you will not see in mainstream Isshinryu however, is the subtle posturing that must occur in order to activate these mirrored motions.

Bilateral actions of the limbs, such as a right or left middle block, are not performed the same. In Seisan kata, for example; the block/punch/punch/kick punch sequence is performed three times. The first sequence should be done with a slip step, followed by a retracting left middle block. The second sequence should be done without a slip step with a slightly extending right middle block. In accord with Kiko principles these nuances will maximize the physical power of the blocks. Failure to add this subtlety will not only remove an added level of power, but could contribute to its failure. However, in mainstream bunkai, such strength differences in applications are seldom noticed because one's training partner or competitor is also moving from the same lack of understanding.

CHALLENGE 14

The sole reason Shimabuku taught

forearm blocks was to spare the arms from

bone-breaking injury by angling the

two forearm bones to absorb the shock

of impact.

REBELLION

This statement only presents half the story.

In the Esoteric Tradition, the ideal forearm block is done on a three-quarter angle, neither vertical, nor flat-sided. The three-quarter middle block supports the deflection of both a vertical and horizontal punch/grab against you. The reason is that a purely flat-sided block (where radius and ulna bones both make contact) is less effective against a horizontal arm attack.

Whether you start your blocking action from the hip chamber, hands hanging at your sides, or from a guard, everyone must choose from one of three starting positions to arrive at the three quarter position; You must either rotate your forearm clockwise or counter-clockwise (however slight), or do the block with no rotation at all. A purely vertical (double-bone, or flat-sided forearm) or horizontal middle block (Radial bone edge) will not masterfully stop the full range of punches that can assault you. Masterful blocking is necessary when you have two skilled, high-level competitors going against one another.

The three-quarter middle block is a superior blocking arm position. From an energetic vantage this forearm angle will better cut through both long range (horizontal punching) and short-range (vertical punching) styles. A bone-edge block is most effective against a full punch, while the two-boned or flat side forearm block is ideal for stopping a vertical punch.

The Esoteric Teachings insist that how you enter and conclude your engagement with any technique is equally important to the actual moment of contact with another.

CHALLENGE 15

One should develop strong low, middle,

and high blocks.

REBELLION

Surprise!

The traditional low, middle and high blocks are not actually the primary blocks in advanced study.

Since Isshinryu arrived in the United States, catching the American fancy in the late 1960's, most Isshinryu schools taught and still teach the three primary blocks: low, middle, and high as a defensive staple. Western culture embraced this fundamental defense wholeheartedly. Bone edge, flat edge, open-hand and close-fist forearm parries are the norm in most dojos. However, a critical nuance is overlooked at advanced training levels. These blocks are generally executed as part of a two-arm action. The secondary arm, sometimes referred to as the 'inside' arm or 'pass off,' accompanies the primary block. This double arm-blocking action conceals the real intention of the coordinated motion. The inside arm is the true and primary block. The commonly perceived low/middle/high blocks are actually follow-up strikes or joint-lock preparations.

It's not that the three basic blocks cannot or do not work as parries. They are just not the complete story. Watch any full-contact match. Notice how few competitors actually use traditional high, middle or low blocking motions as their defense. They are never or minimally used at best. The traditional blocks are not as practical or realistic as other methods. Yet, in the dojo, a large amount of training time is devoted to their practice.

CHALLENGE 16

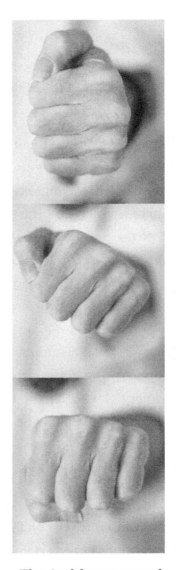

The Isshinryu punch

is a vertical punch.

REBELLION

At an advanced level, it's not that simple.

In the Esoteric Traditions we recognize two types of striking impact, cryptically referred to as *Hard* and *Soft*. Hard strikes refer to the actual body mass behind the impact, how much body weight you put behind your punch or kick. The masters of fist striking just don't just hit with their arms. They hit with their whole body. The difference is extraordinary.

Soft impact refers to the energetic impact to another's body, an event that occurs both prior to and during the physical blow. The Soft impact is, in essence, an electro-magnetic jolt to the opponent's meridian system that enhances the damaging physical strike that follows.

At advanced training levels, punching has a slightly different technical nuance when performed on the right and left sides of the body. This is why the vertical strike of Isshinryu was originally taught to be thrown first on the right side of the body, and launched from a chamber in which the right hand is facing palms inward toward the waist. This creates a subtle clockwise rotation of the fist when it is thrown. This is significant because if the same punch were thrown from the left side as a standalone strike, that is, not part of an alternating drill, it would need to be rotated into a three-quarter downward position to maximize its thrust.

There are professional fist strikers who insist that the proper and advanced way to impact their targets is with a three-quarter, palm-down rotation of the hand. In some cases, this is both anatomically and bioenergetically correct because the energy-gating action from the arm's slight rotation better channels Ki into the deltoid muscle. Rather than engage in a debate as to which fist is better, simply consider that different fist actions cause different energetic effects.

It is far more beneficial to seek the reasons for various fist methods then to flatly claim that one fist is superior to all the others. Every fist configuration has a unique place and purpose in the arts.

In many of the debates over punching effectiveness, I have often observed little commentary on the energetic effects of hand striking. This is an important but missing facet of all fist work, which could benefit the entire martial community. It could also fill in some of the information gaps why one style chooses a particular fist method over another.

We suggest making the debate on the subject more investigative by looking for the best explanation for a fist's existence. In Isshin Kempo we apply an Internal template to understand both why and how different fist strikes affect another's body outside of blunt trauma.

CHALLENGE 17

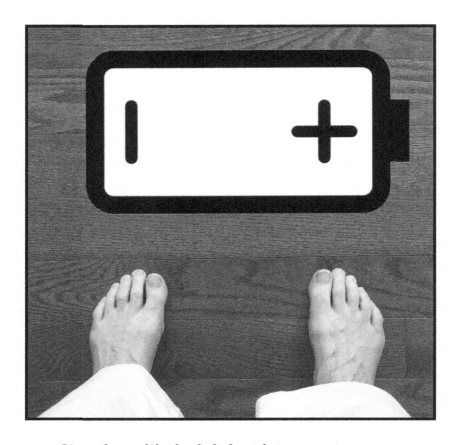

Stepping with the left foot into any stance holds the same value as stepping with the right foot into any stance.

REBELLION

This statement is false.

Regarding practical application, personal preference should not be the prime motivator for which side you chose to step in a kata bunkai. We always want the most advantageous tactic. In the Esoteric Teachings, Ki flows differently between the right and left limb actions. This makes it crucial to step correctly, which means understanding the energy value of each foot action to ensure the success of a masterful technique. A left foot Seisan dachi is most effective stepping to the outside of an opponent's right foot. A right foot is most advantageous stepping to the inside of an opponent's left foot.

The role of the essential Okinawan kata was to preserve the Chinkuchi principles of stancework. In *The Soul Polisher's Apprentice* (2007) I outlined the following:

Some kata rationales regarding the use of specific stances are sorely misleading. How many times have you heard that while standing in a Seisan or Sanchin dachi you should grip your toes? This is somewhat misdirected advice that needs more explanation. One should press the pads of the foot downward, broadening contact to open the Bubbling Springs acupressure point, not grip in such a way that the middle joints of the toes lift off the ground, which has the opposite effect of closing this acupoint point.

In talking exclusively about the feet, we also fall prey to describing the parts to explain the whole. The body/mind connection is a one-piece unit. You cannot move in the physical dimension without affecting the mental realms. You also cannot position your feet without affecting the Ki flow in all your limbs.

Combined with subtle leg and hip positioning, many stances are not one, but a multiple of two separate postures with dual functions. Each dachi or stance is defined by specific weight changes, and the action of stepping. The value of this shifting goes undetected by most Hard stylists and certainly by an opponent with a biomechanical orientation. There is a Yin Seisan dachi and a Yang Seisan dachi, a Yin Neko dachi and a Yang Neko dachi, and so on.

One dachi is a Ki-sending or transmitting posture. The other is a Ki-receiving posture. Whether a stance is in a Yin or Yang mode is not determined solely by the placement of the feet, but by a precise relationship of the limbs to one another, or what we collectively call the Hard gates. The Hard gates are further enhanced with correct breathing patterns and a mental posturing, which we call a *Soft* gate. Correct mental posturing must always accompany the physical form for maximum results.

There are also unique fundamentals to stepping in different directions with the same stance. For example, Gojuryu's Seiuchin kata opens with a Seuichin dachi on a forty-five degree angle. Shimabuku's Seiuchin opens with a ninety degree angle. One method isn't right, the other wrong. From the Kiko perspective a different set of bunkai is being taught. Esoteric Kata reveals these distinctions to help you get it right.

CHALLENGE 18

The Isshinryu fist chamber is a fixed position, formed by placing the palms at the side of the waist.

REBELLION

In kihon practice it is helpful to begin with one fixed, side chamber position. But there are actually multiple fist chambers that include both high and low, forward and rearward, hand positioning. Each chamber serves its own combative purpose and each possesses a specific energetic characteristic. Rebel Isshinryu identifies four hip chambers:

A forward chamber with palms facing the waist.

A forward chamber with palms facing upward.

A rearward chamber with palms facing the waist

A rearward chamber with palms facing upward.

Each chamber is selected on the basis of how to control captured arm energy, and what kind of strike or arm extension best follows. The chamber, referred to as the *hiki-te* or 'returning-hand' often retracts with a captured wrist or elbow, which is then held stationary after being rotated clockwise or counter-clockwise for a counter-offending strike or lock. This act of rotating a captured arm determines in part the chamber position for the fist. The essence of Okinawan karate bunkai was to seize control then strike or further lock up your opponent. A great deal of emphasis was placed upon the best methods for capturing an adversary's arm.

The majority of traditional Okinawan karate styles choose the palms up waist chamber. Tatsuo Shimabuku, the rebel, preferred palms facing inward. His choice reveals a Kiko formula that supports the strength of his selected fist strikes and locks.

95

CHALLENGE 19

All blocks, kicks and punches found in the

Isshinryu kata are clearly defined

by their labels.

REBELLION

Since Isshinryu's introduction into the U.S., serious, long-term Western practitioners have, over the decades, slowly begun to understand that when it comes to comprehending the reason for Asian-created kata, looks can be deceiving. Many of Isshinryu's vertical punches, blocks, and spear-hand strikes are not what they appear at face value. At advanced levels, strikes become blocks, blocks become strikes, and both categories of technique also and often act as set ups for joint locks.

Okinawan sensei understood quite well that a common reaction to a physical engagement was to end up in a close-quarter, grappling/striking contest. The effects of a punch are not always guaranteed. A well-placed, joint lock can offer a greater assurance of success and a better chance of delivering a decisive blow afterward. Hence, one of the primary Okinawan tactics was to first seize control then strike. Isshinyryu kata offer an extensive set of standing, joint-lock bunkai.

CHALLENGE 20

Mid-body spear hand strikes are

designed to penetrate/puncture/damage

body tissues and organs.

REBELLION

Perhaps, in old world Okinawa, mid-body spear hands were effective strikes, but not in America, where most people only need enough finger strength to push a keypad. In particular, spear hands directed to the torso are serious finger injuries waiting to happen.

When people made their living fishing, farming and toiling off the land, their hands were exceptionally strong. Today, typing or slinging the pen does not a samurai make. In addition, the old world use for the spear hand was not exclusively intended for body-jabbing or body-puncturing, save for hitting the eyes or for advanced pressure point work. Rather, the spear had another primary and practical purpose.

According to research, modern society, in just one generation, has seen a twenty percent loss of grip strength. And our ability to grip has been weakening for millions of years. Many students do not even have the time to properly train their fingers to damage the torso of an opponent. The more likely result is injury to the fingers and the loss of an effective weapon in your arsenal.

We must therefore ask if the fingers were primarily used to strike the torso or pressure points. We think neither application defines the spear hand's primary function. We believe the spear hands were used to gain a grappling advantage. A spear hand allows easy access to slip your arm between an opponent's arm and torso to gain control of their elbow.

This use for the spear hand gives anyone a practical and tactical advantage over another's body by making it a viable set up for a joint lock or controlling move. This is a far more functional rationale for spear hand use and it can be employed by anyone at any skill level.

Mid-body spears should be performed as rising motions to insert between another's arm and torso to create a controlling gap. Just as a round peg does not fit through a square hole, a fist's knobby size would not fit as easily between someone's arms pressed into their waist.

In the Esoteric Traditions a spear hand is also considered an 'open' or 'soft' hand. It is used in Kiko as a means of transmitting energy to and from another by either tapping, striking, brushing, rubbing or simply passing nearby the opponent's body. In the Internal arts, it is also noted that opening your hand from a closed-hand position creates a specific energy dynamic, while simply keeping your hand open allows for easy transfer of energy to and from another's body. These 'spearing' movements were employed to penetrate or puncture another's energy field to manipulate their Ki. Energy manipulation is more effective when the extended fingers are neither too relaxed, nor too stiff.

CHALLENGE 21

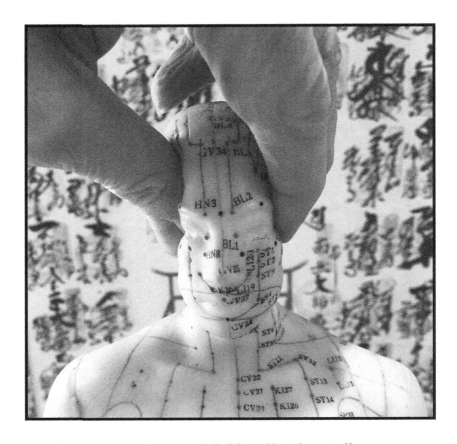

Pressure points are highly effective strikes.

Isshinryu kata are filled with many

point-related targets.

REBELLION

Pressure point study is fascinating. It is also dangerous. If pressure points are so effective in karate, why weren't they historically conveyed in everyone's kata training? And if they were part of advanced training in Isshinryu, the evidence in the modern dojo suggests that few practitioners were ever taught this facet of their art.

The Japanese call their pressure point art *kyusho-jitsu* (vital point technique). *Kyusho* training isn't a simple strike-by-the-numbers art, where you effortlessly hit a point and watch your adversary fall helplessly to the ground. Most seminar demonstrators select passive subjects to demonstrate their knock outs. Live opponents fight back with their own threatening skill sets. Also, some people appear less susceptible, even impervious, to pressure points strikes.

Kiko is considered a more advanced study than pressure point striking because it reveals the underlying system behind pressure point effectiveness. With advanced Kiko skills one can also seal the channels against many pressure point attacks.

Interestingly, there was little to no commentary about pressure points from the first generation, U.S. Isshinryu teachers in the early years of the system's arrival in the United States. Pressure point theory and technique did not gain significant traction in the United States until the early 1990's, mostly due to the work of the Kyushu Jitsu expert, George Dillman, who might be considered America's, 'Father of modern pressure-point striking'. The Puerto Rican Isshinryu sensei, Javier Martinez, was one of the first Isshinryu teachers to publicly release research on the pressure points in the Isshinryu kata in a series of small but informative books published in the mid-to-late 1990's.

Pressure point striking is an extension of Kiko principles. Both methods work from the bio-energetic platform. Kiko could be likened to the alphabet, and Pressure Point striking to words chosen from the letters of that alphabet. This Energy Alphabet has not been made available to mainstream martial artists. Even pressure point work remains a study by a minority of practitioners. One study however, can lead to the other.

The deepest level one can go in the martial arts is into the core energy currents of physical movement. This is where many of the tried and true masters dwelled and why we attribute to them such extraordinary talent. The Philosopher, Arthur Schopenhauer, once commented about 'talent' saying, *"Talent hits a target no one else can hit; Genius hits a target no one else can see."*

There's genius buried in the Isshinryu kata. Both Kiko and pressure point knowledge is there for the asking.

CHALLENGE 22

Isshinryu teachers are well aware

how and why the Sanchin kata

represents the *"essence of karate."*

REBELLION

There is a fair amount of myth, misunderstanding and miscommu-
nication about Sanchin's potential, both within the Isshinryu community and the larger sphere of Okinawan karate systems in general. This has minimalized the Esoteric nature of this potent form.
We can add to this the confusing fact that multiple ryu execute
Sanchin quite differently. As a result, many students are being led
astray about this pattern. When pressed for explanations, there
are sensei who recite the Nike quip, *"Just do it."* If you want to
learn how to drive a car for the first time, fly a plane or scuba dive,
how comfortable will you feel if the instructor says, "Just do it?"

Making guttural rasping breath sounds, with vein popping,
ego-stroking, muscular contraction for the express purpose of
displaying one's physique is a far cry from what Sanchin's true
practice seeks to convey.

Sanchin offers students a pre-eminent martial blueprint, which
was Chojun Miyagi's design and hope. Despite much literature to
the contrary, this Form's fundamentals were carefully constructed
to train the body's Biofield or Subtle Energies. This wasn't the language of the ancients. They called their inner training, Chi Kung,
Chinkuchi, Kiko or Internal training.

CHALLENGE 23

An intelligent design went into the

selection of Tatsuo's eight Isshinryu kata.

The rationale is clear to its teachers.

REBELLION

Unfortunately, Tatsuo Shimabuku did not leave us with detailed commentary on this particular subject. In fact, the mainstream karate community appears to lack a concise definition why any martial kata curriculum chooses to sequence their patterns in the manner they do. We need more in-depth conversation about the value and order of the Isshinryu kata.

Do you think it would make much of a difference if you were taught Seiuchin kata first, followed by Seisan kata?

Probably no other kata is so controversial in regard to its placement in a traditional curriculum than the Sanchin form. It is taught first in the Uechi and Goju systems, but last in Isshinryu. It was a primary kata taught to Okinawans who trained in Fukien, China with some styles emphasizing its muscular tensions, some it's breathing, some its grappling potential, and some its ballistic potential.

Exerpt from *The Soul Polisher's Apprentice*, (Goedecke):

The three forms *Seisan, Seiuchin* and *Neihanchi* teach the internal relationships of the three primary stances of the same names to the rest of the limbs. The kata, *Wansu, Chinto*, and *Kusanku*, present internal lessons of the intermediate and advanced-level stances. Stance distinctions represent one of the first layers of internal teachings. Our feet act as ground wires. Changing our foot postures from a Cat to a Horse stance, for example, enhances specific types of parries, strikes, locks, and set-ups. I am not referring to a stance's mechanical, leveraging, or locomotive function. Rooting or grounding ourselves with the proper stance allows us to firmly hold our territory, to immobilize an opponent, or to neutralize different types of energy strikes, much like a lightening rod grounds a lightening strike. By contrast, some stances lift and lighten, enabling greater mobility. There are also lessons to be found in both the still feet and moving feet of a form. Seisan kata, the first form in most Isshin syllabi, teaches the energetics of the parallel foot stances: that is, standing postures where your feet have a parallel relationship to one another. We call these stances the *neutral* postures. Neutral postures are defined as having an equal Ki flow up and down the legs. Seiuchin kata instructs us in the energetics of the symmetrical, outward-turned stance of the same name. This posture pulls Ki downward. Neihanchi kata instructs us in the energetics of the inward turned feet, which channel energy up into the trunk to support back strength. Seisan, seiuchin, and neihanchi kata make up the Shimabuku's original kata sequence. Advanced footwork of the non-symmetrical, unequal, weight-distributed foot positions like the cat, reverse cat, and reverse t-stances are found in the later kata. Primary stances were taught first; advanced, unequally weighted stances, second. A posture like the cat stance is initially ineffective for a beginner.

There is evidence that both the Classic and Traditional forms are degrading from misinterpretation and/or faulty transmission. One can also never assume there is a pure transmission of any kata from teacher to student.

Knowledgeable instructors of tai chi, for example, will often point out the specific postures critical for the unimpeded flow of chi, but non-traditional, modern, or Hard stylists usually downplay or overlook this level of specificity in the Forms.

In the alphabet of Internal Energy work we see the foundational principles upon which kata applications optimally function. Kata without a partner is worthless if you do not know what to look for. We can also know something of kata's original intention through its outer design.

Regardless of the original purpose behind kata, men will throw their best efforts into divining intelligent applications. The West has produced a colorful diversity of insight regarding their martial arts, which the Japanese refer to as *henka-waza*. If men can turn weapons into ploughshares they will certainly find a way to shape their kata into worthy expressions of their material and/or spiritual needs. According to Northwestern University Professor David Zarefsky, 'That we have such curiosity and controversy is healthy. It keeps our minds alert and challenged. Controversies open up alternative possibilities. They remind us that the things we think are true could be otherwise and they open up new ways of thinking. They make clear the implications of taking a choice. When we resolve controversy we often loose sight of the road not taken. When we do reach conclusions we need to be careful that we don't reach them prematurely or that we don't hold them so rigidly that we are not open to new information.'

Centuries of martial artists have seen the great forms march into the future with more or less definition and value. There are those who will find deep meaning in kata's solo practice, others in its simple kick/punch or grappling interpretations, and still others who will delight in its inner dimensions. Such is the way of men. It's all a matter of perspective and determination. This kaleidoscope of human perception is ever focusing. What meaning or value emerges tomorrow is anyone's guess.

As I delved into the internal rationalizations behind the Isshin kata, it gradually became clear why Shimabuku's kata syllabus started with a Seisan, Seiuchin and Neihanchi lineup. Isshin Kempo founder, W.S. Russell, did not start with this sequence. He taught in order; Seisan, Seiuchin, Wansu, Neihanchi. With hindsight, I see that Russell was not aware of the specific internal organizations being conveyed in each form.

Also, martial historians have questioned the appearance of later Okinawan kata. Newer, additional forms were appearing in the late 1800-1900's. Some historians feel that as Japan took center stage in the martial arts after Funakoshi's presentation to Emperor Hirohito, the Okinawan karate masters felt the need to secure and thus promote the legitimacy of an ancient martial heritage to their arts to prevent the Japanese from getting all the attention. In their attempt to promote the arts some misleading propaganda about the depth and scope of these fighting systems was put forth.

In a nutshell: seven of the eight kata are applied combat forms. The eighth kata, *Sanchin*, stands out as an internal, energy cultivator. It is used to develop extraordinary strength by means of activating internal principles that are then added to the biomechanical strengths and performance of the other seven forms. Think of Sanchin as the hub of a wheel whose spokes represent conduits feeding energy principles to the remaining seven fighting forms.

Seisan: involves practice of the neutral stances/gates, balancing Yin/Yang actions and setting up a fundamental formula for understanding how the body's energy polarity reverses during change of directions.

Seiuchin: practice of the Yin stances/gate

Neihanchi: practice of Yang stances/gates and the rotational power of the torso.

Wansu: Often highlighted for its one throwing technique, and informally called the 'Dumping' form, this kata actually explores the nuances of a half-dozen takedowns and locks from close-quarter clinches.

Chinto: offers us advanced understanding of the energy affects of the Cat and Reverse-Cat stances.

Kusanku: Alongside its ground grappling solutions, this kata investigates the energy effects of spiraling actions found in its many turns.

Sunsu: Although commonly described as a collection of various sets from other Isshinryu kata, this observation is not entirely true. (See Challenge #56)

Sanchin: A premiere Kiko, energy-cultivating form.

More digging remains to be done by Isshinryu's next generation to further unlock ever more meaningful rationales for each of the Isshinryu kata.

CHALLENGE 24

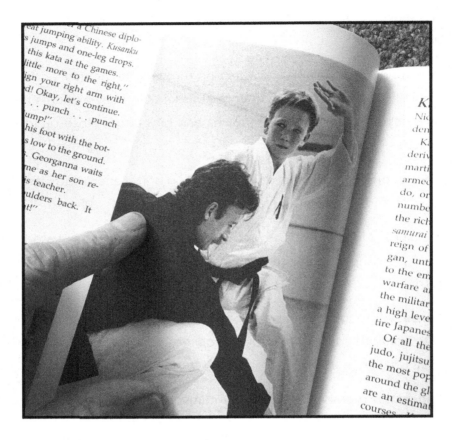

Change your kata when necessary to meet your personal comfort level. Your body knows how it wants to move.

REBELLION

This statement conveys only the most rudimentary truth.

There's no point doing a kata sequence over and over if you can't perform or apply it properly due to injury or personal anatomical challenges.

I've taught students with structural anomalies and injuries that prevented them from doing a kata the way Shimabuku taught. In these cases, the challenging moves must be adapted to the student's physical issues.

Personal comfort or preference however, should never be the reason to permanently alter a kata movement or sequence. I've had adult students tell me that doing a cat stance was "stupid," or they refused to tuck their pelvis forward because, "It felt gay." One student added a personal flourish to his middle block, quipping, "This is how *my* body wants to move." Another, after seven years of training told me, "Oh! You mean you want me to move the way you are showing, not the way I want to move." Modern sensei face many uphill battles when teaching the essence of karate form.

If you beat your competitor, it doesn't mean you possess the ultimate form or technique. It simply means your adversary wasn't as good as you. Both of you could still be sub par. One has to be careful not to alter a Traditional pattern without a clear understanding of its higher or originally intended purpose. Yet, some students and teachers will never come to know the depth of lessons inherent in their own kata.

A student named Dan met a one-year jujitsu practitioner who de-valued the practice of Traditional karate forms. He encouraged Dan to "innovate" his techniques. This jujitsu student's illusion was that he himself, with so little time in training, did not have any real grasp on his own fledgling techniques enough to innovate them. The central purpose of kata is to pass along what had already been innovated to a high degree.

A female *yudansha* in Okinawan karate enrolled in her College, Tang So Do school. Her new teacher instructed a beginner to stand across from her and throw strikes. As the defender, she was told, "find a way to block or deflect the attacks". A creative exercise no doubt, but this is not effective teaching.

The in-depth bunkai manual was not passed to many first gener-ation teachers of Okinawan or Japanese kata. This created a wall of limitation to the interpretations, which were then passed on to successive generations. Western culture received basic kata interpretation 101 in the early days because there wasn't enough time to grasp the advanced language of kata bunkai. Even today we have both students and instructors guessing about kata appli-cations.

CHALLENGE 25

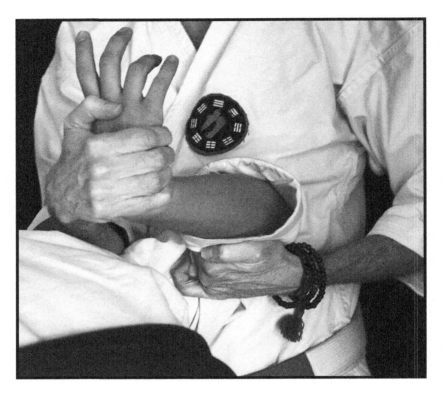

Isshinryu is an ineffective system against ground grapplers.

REBELLION

The Okinawans were well aware that fights often ended up both close-quarter and/or on the ground. Advanced Isshinryu bunkai offers many tactics and techniques to check an adversary who seeks to unbalance you and take you down. Isshinryu kata contain standing lock submissions, grappling counter-strikes and other anti-grappling defenses in its advanced bunkai.

Isshinryu's earliest introduction into the U.S. focused mainly on ballistic motions, striking with all parts of the body. Over the recent decades however, a shift has occurred in Isshinryu's combative tactics. We see emerging revelations in curriculums of highly effective, close-quarter grappling skills that more closely approximate a realistic violent, civilian encounter.

During World War II the man responsible for training the British Commandos, Major W.E. Fairbairn, instructed his soldiers to avoid ever taking the enemy to the ground. Fairbairn was assigned to one of the toughest police forces in the world, the Shanghai Municipal Police where he organized the famous Shanghai Riot Squad and developed his lethal fighting system.

The Okinawan masters would have agreed with Fairbairn's stand-and-fight tactic. Although ground grappling is an excellent skill, major factors are often overlooked when considering it as an effective means of civil defense. Fighting in an uncluttered space on matted floors does not reflect how damaging and punishing the surrounding environment can be.

CHALLENGE 26

Everyone gets the pure, unadulterated

kata from their teacher.

REBELLION

Chances are the martial information students receive today was altered during its transmission from its succession of teachers beginning with Tatsuo Shimabuku before arriving at your teacher's doorstep for you to try on.

There is a common phenomenon in martial arts instruction that when ideas are transmitted they have a tendency to 'drift' from the original content or context. That is, they can easily veer away from the original meaning, even with the best intention to maintain the purity of the movement. This can happen innocently, for instance, as a result of choosing a different emphasis for a technical set to make a point. A student may practice with the new emphasis and forget the original move.

Every Isshinryu student is caught in the tide of his or her instructor's teaching perspective. There is no guarantee that your teacher's kata or your kata hasn't drifted. We all have to start our study somewhere but the question is, whether this drift is limiting or liberating.

CHALLENGE 27

The early Asian martial way of 'don't ask,

just do,' is the best method of training.

REBELLION

For centuries the general teaching method of Asian masters was highlighted by a philosophy of 'just do as I do.' Hard practice was preferred over 'empty' talk. But the result of this silence has led to a scarcity of verbal articulation regarding advanced levels of training in many martial art systems exported to the Western culture. Add to this the dojo protocol of 'not asking questions of one's seniors,' a trait believed influenced by the Japanese Samurai culture, along with the wall of ego that can go up between some teachers and students, and you have a recipe for serious limitations in explaining advanced training stages.

It's time for martial students and teachers to speak up when appropriate and ask more probing and pertinent questions. Traditional karate training in the United States is on the wane. Form training is receding. This is not a failure within the Traditional systems themselves. The information is mostly good, but a more grounded presentation of kata practice could benefit the Traditional arts. Kata's presentation is not grabbing the interest of modern students the way it did in the early 1970's when karate was fresh and exciting. If Isshinryu is going to survive the future it will need to ramp up its appeal, value, and dynamism to the general public. Father Shimabuku may have been right for his time, but we've been at the tipping point of a new era of thinking and will need to re-evaluate the role of the martial arts in the 21st century.

Tae Kwon Do took the U.S. by storm in the 1970's followed by MMA (Mixed Martial Arts) in the 80's. Both systems changed the face of the American martial landscape. Thousands of instructors in karate systems worldwide began to rethink, regroup, and better anchor their kata performance and bunkai to stronger rationales and more relevant purpose. We need to keep this process moving forward.

If we take a quick look at the arc of martial arts in the United States, Judo was the first martial sport imported into the U.S. resulting from returning servicemen in WWII. Judo reigned strongly from the early 1950's until the mid-1960's. Karate followed with its exotic, powerful, crisp kicks and punches. Various forms of Kung fu, Tai Chi, Aikido, Ninjitsu, followed. All had a shot at stardom in the early 1970's. But there were simply not enough teachers of these disciplines in the West to meet either the demand or the curiosity at that time. Tae Kwon Do, with its focus on spectacular kicking, and emphasis on sport competition, stole the scene from the Japanese and Okinawan striking arts during the 1970's to become the darling of the industry, while Kickboxing emerged to satisfy the public's general bloodlust for realistic fighting. Beginning in the 1980's, the contact arts began to fuse kick-boxing, boxing, wrestling, jujitsu and all the other Asian striking arts into the MMA, Mixed Martial Arts movement, which provided a bonanza for the martial industry as it drew a wide range of spectators. Along with the action film industry, the MMA brought martial awareness into the mainstream American consciousness with a host of dynamic competitors hailing from all fighting styles and systems.

The monastic martial arts and the Esoteric Teachings remained on the sidelines quietly advancing a small, but dedicated sector of the U.S. martial population.

CHALLENGE 28

If Shimabuku didn't teach it,

it is not Isshinryu.

REBELLION

Isshinryu has outgrown its creator and evolved far more than what you or I, or any single Isshinryu sensei, even its founder, taught. Collectively, the multi-national children and grandchildren of Isshinryu are now carrying the system to greater fields of possibility.

At this time in the U.S. we have seen the passing of many first generation American teachers. Second generation teachers have or are now reaching their teaching zenith as well. Third and fourth generation teachers are exerting their emerging influence. Isshinryu's legacy has collectively exceeded its founder. Isshinryu masters from around world are claiming Isshinryu for their own by putting their personal stamp on their curriculums. This is not denigrating or dishonoring the source, but enhancing and challenging Isshinryu's value to meet changing times. Those early 1950's seeds have since spread across the globe and are blossoming in foreign soil with completely different cultural values.

This evolution began early with the expansion of Tatsuo's Isshinryu into Ungi Uezu Isshinryu, Kichiro Shimabuku Isshinryu, and in the U.S. with such leaders as Advincula Isshinryu, Long and Wheeler Isshinryu. Don Nagle Isshinryu etc,. No two adepts will carry Isshinryu forward the same. Not a single one of them. Some nuance, some new and fresh, revitalized or reworked perspective, will find itself through the new venue, and a new class of student will arise. Isshinryu is in a state of constant change. Uezu added sport kicks, Gary Alexander, of Isshinryu Plus, eliminated the knee drops in Kusanku. The late Don Nagle (1938-1990) maintained the old way of middle blocking after Shimabuku changed it to a straight wrist.

Pressure points were added or uncovered, certainly exposed, by George Dillman and his Isshinryu disciples. England's, Ian Abernathy's call to revisit karate bunkai reveals many more joint locks inherent our forms. Monastic insights reveal a strong Buddhist influence in all of Okonawan's karate kata construction. Kiko practices reveal Isshinryu's rich, chi-kung layer. The history of Isshinryu's evolution goes on.

There are many Isshinryu instructors who favor different sets or arrangement of *bunkai* (application) because it benefits their body makeup or logic scheme. No Isshinryu overlord will magically appear in your dojo and exact a fine if you're not doing the moves exactly the way Tatsuo Shimabuku intended them to be done. Certain egos may call you on the carpet if you are a member of a larger organization, but you probably signed onto their regime for their critique.

Years ago an interesting phenomenon occurred while I was surveying American instructors about their martial arts systems. I asked various teachers to outline the major points of their teaching curriculums. Strangely, very few chose to answer this part of the survey. Their lack of response perplexed me. Why wouldn't they want to talk about their martial passion? I concluded that it was more likely they were teaching it differently from their teachers and did not want an authoritarian hammer to drop on them and have to answer for veering from the general game plan.

I challenge anyone to tell me that they are doing Isshinryu exactly the way Shimabuku did it down to a 'T'. Even with the best intention of doing so, it's just not human nature. It's even difficult to get out of bed and duplicate your morning routine from the day before—*exactly*. How are we supposed to believe that every sensei is conveying Shimabuku's entire system exactly the way he intended it? It's an uncontestable fact that Shimabuku himself was making modifications to his style as it was developing up to the day he died. Change is constant. The question is, are the changes Shimabuku's followers made and are making, upgrading, downgrading, or maintaining the status quo of the art?

Tatsuo's Isshinryu is the source system and he is the undisputed father of the specific martial knowledge and insights he formed to birth his own style.

However, in rare cases, some instructors force their students to suspend reality by erecting a wall of mystique when asking them to engage in practices that make little sense. Even stranger are sensei who suspend their own common sense with the erroneous idea that that they are getting the real teaching believing that if you do not understand it, it must be great! This is why they call it *inscrutable* Asian wisdom.

Dan, a ten-year plus Isshinryu student, listened to his teacher, a long-term East Coast karate sensei, explain a bizarre breathing pattern to accompany his Sanchin kata. A post-graduate, PHD student, Dan simply could not comprehend his sensei's method. He could not perform, it no less explain it coherently to me. In another instance, this same student was told never to pivot on the heel of his foot during a Seisan kata move. I asked him why he was given this explicit advice. He wasn't sure. We proved this advice was wrong for the bunkai he'd been told to perform. Dan returned to his teacher open-minded enough and suggested his sensei ask his teachers for clarification. Dan's sensei remarked, "No way. They will listen to my question, punch me in the face, and walk away." Seriously? This is Sandbox 101, control by fear. Okay, we hope this was an isolated case of the blind leading the blind—but these were senior East coast instructors.

Another one of my students sat in on a class given by an Isshinryu, seventh dan who woo'd his advanced students by telling them that they could block a strike, not only on the inside of the punching arm, but also on the outside. No wonder the old masters are rolling their eyeballs in their graves at all the over-inflated American high dan rank awards. Someone once observed that there were more tenth dans in New Jersey than all of Okinawa! Perhaps we are really good—at deceiving ourselves.

There is a concerted attempt within the Isshinryu community to preserve and to practice the best principles of the ryu. This is a laudable action. Sound principles are the alphabet of all the martial arts. However, when I look at the principles inherent in Isshinryu I see an unfinished work in Shimabuku's martial career. What understanding might this master have arrived at had he lived another twenty years? Today's sensei will be the ones who answer that question and continue his work.

CHALLENGE 29

Everyone knows the reason why certain

kata moves change in cadence.

REBELLION

In an interview, years ago, with East Coast, Gojuryu master, Anthony Mirakian (1933-2015), a long term, respected senior Meibukan practitioner, former head of this system in the U.S., Mirakian stated that it was more common to witness kata with variable speeds and pauses in Okinawan kata then today's often rush-through performances. The cadence of old world kata was not set to one speed. Master Mirakian knew Tatsuo Shimabuku personally. These rhythmic shifts, performed during a kata, are the strongest confirmation of Esoteric principles inherent in Okinawan karate because, from a combative standpoint, you are not going to stop or slow down during a fight. So what is happening? Why do we see slow and fast motions?

Two theories address the fast and slow movements in kata. The first suggests that a slow movement indicates either a pull or pressing motion where strong body resistance will be met. For instance, if you deflect an arm, then grab and pull it to set your adversary up for a lock or strike, the slow motion limb action during the kata indicates you are pulling a resistant mass.

The second theory is part of the Esoteric Teachings. The cadence deals with Ki flow during physical actions. Kata taught with fast then slow movements are designed to create a backlog or energy vacuum to enhance the strength of the next move in the kata sequence. An entire set performed slowly in one direction and faster in another has to do with the lunar, solar and geomagnetic field effects upon the meridian channels of the body. Certain compass directions require a specific speed to maintain or increase physical strength.

In the Seisan kata we have a hook-blocking action followed by a slow retraction of the hooking arm. If you hook another's punch then pause briefly before turning your hand over to grab it, you will more effectively affect the energy of the opponent than if you perform the entire set quickly. This seemingly innocuous pause will give you noticeable control over the grabbed limb and the ability to pull it with less effort.

CHALLENGE 30

All front kicks are done with the

ball of the foot.

REBELLION

A front kick with the ball of the foot is unquestionably effective for striking certain targets, but kicking with the shin is simply devastating, while at the same time protecting the toes and small bones of the foot from damage. Many kicks can also be performed more effectively with the cutting shin of the foreleg. Muay Thai kick boxers know this technique well.

In advanced training the so-called 'front' kicks are used for means other than a ball of the foot strike as well. The retraction of a kicking leg can be used as a takedown to bring a close-quarter opponent to the ground.

The foot in a front kick may also be rotated slightly outward to allow for a wider striking surface for hyper-extending another's knee joint or for delivering an incapacitating heel strike to the thigh.

CHALLENGE 31

Breathing has little effect on physical strength other than to supply the muscles with needed oxygen.

REBELLION

Proper breath control has an enormous impact on physical strength.

Like the Yogis of India, the masters of Okinawan karate went to great lengths to understand the value of respiration on the strength systems of the body.

> **Experiment:** Face a wall in a strong stance to push into the wall with the palms of your hands on the wall at chest height. Press firmly into the wall while breathing out. Note how much pressure you can exert and how your palms feel while contacting the wall's surface. Next, do the exact same push again, this time inhaling. You will not be able to contact the wall as firmly.

An exhale charges the extensor muscles allowing for a harder push. An inhale charges the opposite musculature, the flexors, which is why your hands feel like they can't press with the same intensity or force. Tests conducted indicate that when the proper breath cycle is aligned with a karate technique, strength can be dramatically magnified up to 50%. This is why old world masters taught specific breathing patterns to accompany their kata movements.

Proper breath control organizes respiration to manipulate the strength channels to give any karate technique maximum power. Breath control, in this context, has less to do with simply how long or short, slow or fast, loud or silent, you breathe. Breath practice or *Kokyu Ho* was aimed at aligning respiration with the musculo-skeletal and nervous systems to produce heightened power.

One basic rule for developing your breath control during training is to breathe out through your mouth on techniques that extend away from your body. Breathe in through your nose on techniques that move toward the body core.

The Complete Breath

This breathing exercise, found in both yoga and martial arts, works the entire respiratory musculature. Begin by breathing deep into the belly. Next, continue to fill and expand the middle ribs. Finish your inhalation by lifting and filling your chest. Exhale naturally. Repeat the sequence nine times. Practice daily.

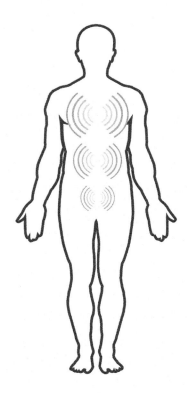

CHALLENGE 32

A Cat stance *(Neko dachi)* is an

important posture

that frees the front leg for kicking.

REBELLION

At face value, the timing between kicking with both feet planted versus one foot forward and raised into a Cat stance is insignificant. The combative rationale for the lead leg's kicking effectiveness is therefore weak. How many full contact matches do you see where the players go into a Cat stance before striking? Few, if any at all. Also, similar to the difference between throwing a jab or a backhand strike, kicking off the lead foot is not the strongest posture to launch a foot strike. It can be used as a surprise maneuver in a self-defense or street encounter. But this is also one of the few postures that we did not see developed in Western combative cultures. The *Neko dachi* is uniquely Asian and it has a much more profound purpose.

The Cat stance is a superior energy-receiving posture. And this stance is almost always paired with a soft, lead arm, open hand action. (Note: There are no moves in any Isshinryu kata that step forward with a Cat stance). Every Cat stance is either stationary, or results from a turning or retreating action. In the second to last move in the Seisan kata sequence the founder has us step back with the right foot into a Cat, coupled with a lead left, open knife-hand block. In the Internal arts, the left side of the body is considered Yin. Yin receives or draws energy inward. This is why the left hand is often held soft (relaxed) or 'receptive' because any tension in the left hand or arm blocks Ki flow. We do not want to short circuit the Ki flow between the players.

Someone throwing a right hand at you will have a lot of energy flowing along their Yin channels down the inside of their arm. Your knife-hand will pick up or bridge that energy as the block nears and contacts the inside of the adversary's arm. Therefore, we want the Soft/Yin channels of the receiving arm to be open/relaxed. The opponent's downward flowing Ki will be received by your upward flowing Ki. For this reason closed hands are rarely used with a retreating or rearward stepping Cat stance.

There is one exception in Seuichin kata. But the principle here is against a two-handed attack. You will need a competent instructor in internal energy work to explain these distinctions.

CHALLENGE 33

Shimabuku once remarked that there was no discernable martial application value to Sanchin kata.

REBELLION

Given that Sanchin is part of Isshinryu's martial curriculum, this statement is a mouthful. If the master's assertion is true, why do we practice the form? Where is Sanchin's value? How does it or should it fit into our training regime?

James Arsenio Advincula, considered to be one of the world's leading experts on Isshinryu karate, once conducted a biometric test in 1997 on Sanchin kata to compare it to callisthenic exertion from a Western exercise perspective. The conclusion; in terms of caloric burn, heart rate conditioning, Sanchin was no different than performing squat thrusts.

This kind of testing however, is far afield from Sanchin's real training value, a secret that has been kept from most Western practitioners—even to this day. Sanchin is a Kiko form. Kiko was the Okinawan equivalent of Chi Kung, the art of manipulating internal energy. The word literally translates as Energy (*Ki*) Breath (*Ko*). The form was designed to train the human Subtle Energy Body, today called the Biofield. Sanchin is a brilliant Ki-training device.

Shimabuku's comment could have meant that although there is no *obvious* martial bunkai there is a less obvious value of tremendous merit—the form's emphasis on cultivating Ki. This notion fits perfectly with the hidden nature of Kiko practice itself. It's not what you see in Sanchin that yields the Form's worth. The value is derived from what is sensed or felt, when you know what to look for. But one has to be initiated into Sanchin's inner realm to both understand and to develop this level of sensitivity.

CHALLENGE 34

The origins of the kata of Isshinryu

have always been *empty-hand*

(weaponless) forms.

REBELLION

The British, Buddhist martial researcher, author and Shaolin karate expert, Nathan Johnson, has done a great service with his historical investigations into the origins of several essential forms selected by Shimabuku for his Isshinryu kata curriculum. Johnson discovered that the Katas, *Sanchin, Seisan* and *Kusanku* were originally sai forms dating back to 14th century Ming dynasty, China. When sai were not available to train with practitioners performed their weapon kata sequences with a combination of closed and open hands, indicating where the sai was to be folded or extended.

This fact must have baffled the early fist masters of Okinawa who tried to make sense out of the weaponless value of these Chinese-influenced forms. What we have then is a kind of kata hybridization or evolution where a once weapon form slowly transformed into an empty-hand or weaponless kata.

It could be theorized that when these forms were adopted by the Okinawans, they had trouble interpreting them. This ambiguity was carried forward into Okinawan Karate bunkai in general, not just with the Isshinryu kata.

Even if Johnson's research was proven incorrect, and Sanchin was indeed a primary empty-hand form, not all Isshinryu instructors possess bunkai for all their kata moves. There is also a wide range of technical interpretations from one school to another.

This perspective makes the martial arts one of the few world disciplines that have passed from generation to generation able to maintain a high degree of ambiguity within some systems.

CHALLENGE 35

The Isshin Code will clarify your training.

REBELLION

The Isshin Code needs decoding.

Codes represent a systematic collection of laws or regulations: a set of conventions governing behavior or activity in a particular sphere; a set of rules and standards adhered to by a society, class.

The Isshinryu Code was influenced by an important Chinese military manual that circulated in the early 17th century, the *Wubei Zhi*; commonly known by its Japanese translation, the *Bubishi* (Master Text). This significant treatise on warfare included a section specifically on empty-hand fighting methods.

In my opinion, there is something irksome about the Isshin Code, which shares similar issues with aspects of the Bubishi. Both are filled, in part, with crypticisms and therefore open to broad interpretation. The Bubishi was obviously not written for the layman or for the average Western-trained martial arts practitioner. Its ambiguity is not unlike the difficulty trying to interpret the applications of Okinawan kata without a guide. I've also encountered many martial artists living in our fast-paced world who don't want to be hampered with academic enigmas or too much detail. Black and white has become the preferred icing.

The Isshin Code represents a set of philosophical observations and homespun Asian wisdom rather than a direct how-to commentary about fighting. It has been suggested these observations were an effort to establish a symbolic code of ethics linking it to the Buddhist Eightfold path. Given that students come to the dojo to learn karate, it would be helpful if the Isshin code had more definitive links to one's actual training practices.

If I gave the Isshinryu Code to the average, adult U.S. martial artists and asked for an explanation of its meaning, and how it applied to their personal training, I suspect we would get either an enormous range of interpretations or blank-faced stares. This Code offers little practical advice for what to do if someone is about to punch you in the face. Do you think in any way it adds to your success on the mat if you know that the blood circulating in your body is similar to the sun and moon?

I also suspect many Isshinryu practitioners are unfamiliar with this code or haven't given it much thought, save for those of an intellectual nature. I doubt it has taken anything away from their physical routines. So, how does this Code apply to our martial training? Why should we ponder it? It certainly appears to be asking us to reflect upon its philosophical observations.

Revisiting the Isshinryu code

A person's heart is the same as heaven and earth

Vital principles of combat can be found in the patterns of nature because Man and Nature are one and the same.

Since we are applying this statement specifically to Isshinryu practice, let's begin with a definition of the word *'Isshin'*. Mainstream literature can easily misinterpret this word as either 'one heart' or 'one mind.' That is, either it means 'heart' as in 'wholehearted' or 'complete', or it means 'mind'. The Japanese interpretation is 'one mind', referring to the 'universal mind,' which in Buddhism pervades all appearance—the Buddha-mind.

In the context of Okinawan and Chinese martial arts, the Heart and Mind were viewed as one and the same. In earlier Asian cultures the concept of the heart/mind was a single unit of being.

We can deduce from this Code's first observation that humans possess similarities to the broader cycles of existence. We contain all the elements of the narrow and the broad, the micro and the macro, the high and the low, the refined and the crude, the skilled and the unskilled. We are, in essence, our own miniature galaxies with our own interactive cycles and patterns of behavior similar to the larger world surrounding us. Our martial actions are therefore bound to the same principles binding Heaven and Earth.

The Chinese refer to the interplay of these patterns and principles as the Yin and the Yang (Jap. *In* and *Yo*) If you are going to defeat your opponent you need to look closely and candidly at your opposition's martial behavior as well as your own patterns. You and your opponent will move in a certain fight rhythm. Figuring these patterns out, and not telegraphing your pattern, can work greatly to your advantage.

The blood circulating is similar to the Moon and Sun

Your Ki (life-energy) flows with observable behaviors that both strengthen and weaken. Choose the most favorable cycle.

Blood is also a term synonymous with Ki flow. Ki moves through the body following certain patterns/cycles. The sun rises and falls, the moon waxes and wanes, etc. This statement is relevant to human cycles and the tidal nature of Ki flow in and around the body. These underlying cycles became the basis for the practice-within-a-practice referred to in old Okinawan Hogen language as Chinkuchi, or Kiko. Chinkuchi is the management of the tidal flow

153

of one's life-blood (Ki) particularly for gaining an advantage over an adversary.

Just as a doctor learns to distinguish the properties of a healthy circulation, a martial artist learns to recognize his or her Ki cycles, when they are Yin-charged and when they are Yang-charged. Because this is not part of Western martial education, a qualified teacher will be necessary to point out these distinctions.

The manner of drinking and spitting is either hard or soft

The give and take during any physical engagement reveals
two distinct sets of martial principles and techniques

Bodily actions can be sorted into two dimensions; the biomechanical (Hard), and the Bioenergetic (Soft). 'Spitting' is synonymous with striking or repelling, and also the manner of releasing Ki. Therefore, a strike can be considered either Hard/biomechanical or Soft/internal. Drinking is synonymous with taking in or receiving. I can grab and pull you into me and I can also absorb your Ki. 'Swallowing' implies taking energy from an outside source into oneself, in this case, from the opponent. The Hard approach is to actually draw one physically toward you by seizing a limb. The Soft approach, by contrast, draws the other's Ki into you (actual physical contact is not always necessary). These two complementary actions seek the same desired goal—control.

A person's unbalance is the same as weight.

Your strength or weakness can be determined by
how you use your weight.

This is not a statement about how much you physically weigh. It refers to how you handle both your own body weight and your opponent's. We use our body weight to generate power in three ways: through momentum, leverage and torque. The more weight we muster behind an action, or put behind our moves, the larger the effect. Conversely, if we can't control our own weight, if we don't know how to apply our weight in an organized fashion, we will not be able to avail ourselves of its influence. We can also look at this statement from the standpoint that 'weight' isn't limited to physical mass but can include the 'grip of the mind' on what is needed to accomplish a task. We can therefore throw the weight of our minds into our actions.

Weight is balance. Balance is weight. Unbalance is weight. Weight is unbalance. Weight implies leverage, momentum and rooting. An imbalance in the body diminishes the above three principles. Not getting weight behind your strikes reduces their impact. Not getting weight behind your grappling techniques reduces your leverage. Not getting proper weight behind your stances reduces your resistance and maneuverability, leading to your being uprooted easily. Not getting weight behind your convictions weakens your resolve.

Weight is 'presence'. Lack of weight is lack of presence. Someone said to 'carry weight' means they have a lot of power.

When you are balanced you are carrying your weight appropriately. When you are off balance you have lost control of your potential and are working from a deficit. We generate power in a strike by getting our full body weight behind it. If we are unbalanced we will not be able to get our full weight behind our actions.

There is another level to the idea of getting weight behind your movements. Most students only exert a general control over their weight. In the high end of every martial art there are techniques using body weight that would not be apparent to a layperson. There are masters of many disciplines whose technical knowledge makes them feel much heavier, denser, or more powerful then their actual scale weight might indicate.

The body should be able to change motion at any time

If you are fluid and flexible enough in both mind and body
you will be able to adapt quickly to changing circumstances.
A body (and mind) that cannot change motion when necessary
will suffer mental or physical impediments.

The body doesn't always change its motion when it could benefit from doing so. The culprit behind this inflexibility is often the result of over-conditioning, stuck kinetic patterns, like fixated training ideas or habitual behavior. You must strive to be mentally pliable and physically supple at all times. You must keep your body relaxed. Avoid irritability, agitation, and work through physical fixations, stiffness or rigidity. Kata practice itself has been challenged and criticized as a fixed pattern that does not match the reality of a constantly changing fight scenario. Proponents of this anti-kata idea simply do not understand kata's purpose. Kata is a combat reference of foundational techniques and principles. It should be viewed like a dictionary, rather than a declarative fight sentence. When you learn the principles of a technique in kata you free yourself from the rigidity of adhering to any one technique or set of techniques. When you understand the underlying principle, your technique will become creative and spontaneous. Never dampen or eliminate the possibility of spontaneity as its own inherent power. The value of spontaneous versus rigid patterning is measured in the degree of efficiency generated in each state. Always strive to find the most efficient state.

Strike when the opportunity presents itself

There are five strategic considerations
to capitalize on opportunity.

The first challenge is to actually recognize the moments when opportunity presents itself. In *jiu-kumite* (free-sparring) there is a developmental sequence that almost every novice experiences. After you've geared up, paired with a partner, and begin to *kumite*, you suddenly see an opening, an exposed target on your partner's body. You make a decision what technique to throw. You mentally prepare yourself to execute your move when you realize that the opening has closed before your hand or foot has reached the target. Opportunity lost! How do you capitalize on these moving opportunities?

One person's opportunity is another's loss. Opportunity will appear on five distinct levels of your art; in your selection of specific martial tools, tactics, strategy, state of mind, and in the influence of raw energy patterns coursing through your body (See: Internal Karate: *Mind Matters and the Seven Gates of Power,* Wind School 2014) The last category refers to Internal martial training. You need concrete methods in every category to fully progress. By organizing the components of each category correctly you can learn to leverage any situation to your advantage.

The eye must see every way

The ear must listen in all directions
Hone and attune all your senses toward resolving conflict

'See' and 'hear' is broadly meant as 'sense.' When we are advised to open our senses and refine our proprioceptors the question arises. How many directions and how many dimensions exist for us to direct our senses toward?

Below is a personal meditation I have found helpful in opening the senses and for examining topics of concern and conflicts in both my martial and daily life. This meditation will awaken many latent sensitivities. I call it the Five Star Meditation. This meditation will condition you to see and hear in an ever-widening sphere of influence.

Each Star of the meditation consists of three parts; Physical, Emotional and Spiritual. Start with any part of the meditation that calls to you. This is a rich practice.

THE FIVE STAR MEDITATION

LOOK FORWARD

Physical meditation: Literally look at what is directly in front of you. Take in as much detail as possible. Trace all the objects and motions in your field of vision. Make no judgment. Simply note what you see. Go for detail.

Emotional meditation: Within your field of view note what feels good, pleasant, curious, displeasing. What are you drawn to? What do your eyes avert? How strongly do you connect to what you see of your immediate world?

Spiritual meditation: Peer into your future. Project your imagination in detail for how you wish to see your future self. This practice will pave the way to your deepest desires.

LOOK BACKWARD

Physical meditation: Literally turn around and look behind you. Take in as much detail as possible. Trace all the objects and motions in your field of vision. Make no judgment. Simply note what you see. Go for detail.

Emotional meditation: Within your field of view note what feels good, pleasant, curious, displeasing. What are you drawn to? What do your eyes avert?

Spiritual meditation: Look back into your past. Retrace your significant life steps. Did you make any wrong turns or misassumptions that you could remedy now?

LOOK RIGHT AND LEFT

Physical meditation: Literally take in the periphery on both sides of you. Take in as much detail as possible. Trace all the objects and motions in your field of vision. Make no judgment. Simply note what you see. Go for detail.

Emotional meditation: Within your field of view note what feels good, pleasant, curious, displeasing. What are you drawn to? What do your eyes avert?

Spiritual meditation: What do you strongly connect with in your field of vision? What things or ideas not currently part of your inner vision might actually expand it?

LOOK ABOVE

Physical meditation: Literally look above your head. Take in as much detail as possible. Trace all the objects and motions in your field of vision. Make no judgment. Simply note what you see. Go for detail.

Emotional meditation: Within your field of view note what feels good, pleasant, curious, displeasing. What are you drawn to? What do your eyes avert?

Spiritual meditation: What are your highest aspirations? Possibilities may exist that you are not aware of. Find the most competent or experienced people that have embraced your desires and listen to their views.

LOOK BELOW

Physical meditation: Literally look at the ground beneath your feet. Take in as much detail as possible. Trace all the objects and motions in your field of vision. Make no judgment. Simply note what you see. Go for detail.

Emotional meditation: Within your field of view note what feels good, pleasant, curious, displeasing. What are you drawn to? What do your eyes avert?

Spiritual meditation: How connected do you feel to your immediate environment? Don't take things for granted. Look for solutions that might be right under your nose.

CHALLENGE 36

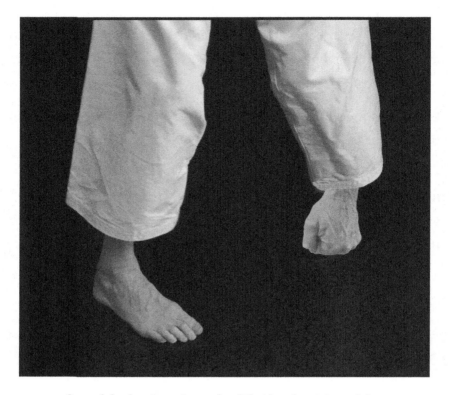

Sanchin is structured with the feet toed-in,

gripping the floor, so you can root

better to the ground.

REBELLION

Isshinryu practitioners have part of this technicality correct, but it appears only a topical understanding.

Is there something about the toe-gripping action that makes the Sanchin stance more doable or rootable than not gripping the floor? If we look specifically at how the Sanchin foot should grip, it is not what you might assume. You must not ball your toes into a fist, as the word 'gripping' suggests. The middle knuckles of the toes should not be raised. The act of toe-gripping in the Sanchin dachi is to pull the toes inward without causing the toe's middle knuckles to bend. This creates more contact with the floor, which opens the Bubbling Springs acupuncture point in the center of the foot. The Bubbling Springs point allows for a greater flow of energy up through the Yin meridians on the inside of the legs, activating them for a greater muscular contraction in the upper body.

What of those other Sanchin considerations like toeing-inward? An important distinction to keep in mind while stepping into Sanchin dachi is that the ball of the foot is not turned inward when concluding the stance. That is a Yang action. Instead, the opposite action must take place. The heel must be pressed or rotated outward—a Yin action. Selecting the wrong method of pivot weakens arm strength. Also, there are different values at play when describing a stationary Sanchin stance versus moving into and out of a Sanchin from the same or different stances. Various hand and arm positioning also effects stance and kicking strength.

Of all the Okinawan dachi, the most misleading propaganda can be found in regard to Sanchin. What exactly is the Sanchin stance?

What is the right way to perform it? And if Sanchin is such an important stance why aren't there more Isshinryu kata using this dachi?

The width you assume for a Sanchin stance can change the body's energy polarity. There is a specific proportionality required for maximum energy flow through the leg meridians affected by Sanchin's foot placement. If you assume a narrow, 'hourglass' Sanchin, both feet should be turned inward to a maximum of 45 degrees, no more than that. Turning the foot beyond 45 degrees does not make a better Sanchin. However, if you assume a wider posture, where the inside of the feet fall to the outside of the shoulders, only the lead foot is to be turned inward.

Martial empiricists cite the reason for the forward foot's inward rotation as a means of providing better 'tensegrity.' That is, this posture gives the body structure as a whole more resilience to forceful pushes and pulls by spreading the force over more of the body. More muscles and skeleton can take the load. The narrowness of the stance however, presents a challenge to this idea. Biomechanically, a wider stance offers more resistance to a push or pull, *unless* you are punching upward.

Stepping into Sanchin requires that the forward foot pivots on the ball to push the heel outward. Do not pick up and turn the ball of the foot inward.

Let's look at the Kiko effect of the Sanchin leg posturing on the Energy Body. Narrow stances, as a rule, concentrate more Ki in the body than wide stances or extended limbs in general. It's easier to concentrate Ki into a condensed physical form. Feet turned inward draw Ki up the Yin channels of the leg (there are three bilateral channels on the inside of each leg. Once the energy is contained in the lower dantien, that Ki (or charge) can be distributed into the arms.

We can't just view the actions of the feet without looking at their effect upon the rest of the body. We are a one-piece unit. So we must also consider the action of crescent stepping. Stationary Sanchin opens up the Yin channels but the crescent step actually pumps the energy upward into the dantien. Crescent stepping is a Ki generator when the step arcs forward in a specific manner and touches down with the ball of the foot first, which is what a toed-in stance forces you to do (touch with the ball of your foot)

Practitioners should note that there are different ways to assume a Sanchin stance: There is both a wide and narrow version of the stance. Kiko reveals even more radical training ideas. Most common Sanchin practice only dwells in the form's base layer. Consider that Sanchin kata itself is also a *concept,* not just a standing posture or sequence of arm motions.

In Shitoryu Sanchin the crescent step is much narrower. The stepping foot only arcs halfway toward the centerline of the body, that is, half the depth of the Isshinryu step. This is a quadrant-specific action. The Isshinryu crescent step, by contrast, arcs all the way front and center of the opposite knee.

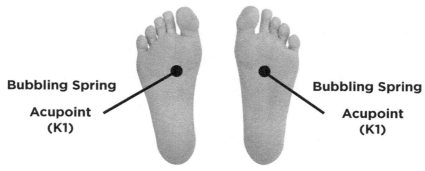

Bubbling Spring

Acupoint (K1)

Bubbling Spring

Acupoint (K1)

CHALLENGE 37

Seisan kata is a beginner kata.

REBELLION

Seisan, like all the other Isshinryu kata, is an advanced and complex form. *Seisan,* literally translated as '13', or in Sanskrit, *'Born of the Three,'* can be performed with far more technical nuance than most people are aware. Isshinryu's kata syllabus represents an extraordinary collection of important Okinawan kata knowledge. Chotoku Kyan, who taught Shimabuku during the 1930's, was a collector of the oldest known island kata. He passed some of these vital forms along to Shimabuku. According to the author, Bruce Clayton in, *Shotokan Secrets*, "...Kyan had gone back to basics by teaching older versions of Okinawan kata instead of the forms modified at Shuri. These kata are preserved in Shimabuku's style, isshin-ryu."

Okinawan martial history draws from three critical sources; the *Naha-te* or Chinese influence and longest running lineage, the *Shuri-te*; a unique methodology of fighting created within and for the Okinawan aristocracy, the *Peichin* samurai, and the Buddhist monastic influence, the least known to the martial public. Deep thought went into the creation of essential Okinawan kata, particularly the three forms; Sanchin, Neihanchi and Seisan. Unraveling the wealth of information in these kata is well worth the investigation. At black belt, I can assure you that you will just be getting started.

CHALLENGE 38

The Isshinryu katas present random,

self-defense sequences.

Sometimes you are just blocking,

sometimes striking, sometimes grappling.

REBELLION

In terms of a live opponent, the way Isshinryu kata bunkai was taught in its early years in the U.S did not resolve every attack but often presented practitioners instead with a random collection of technique. You might block a kick in one sequence or throw a hand strike and trap an arm in another. One could not rely on a start-to-finish conflict resolution in early kata bunkai teaching. Some Isshinryu schools do not even interpret or apply their forms. The kata are just considered 'Traditional' practices, separate from real fighting. The best challenge I once heard from a spectator observing an Isshinryu class, "How come your kata looks completely different from your kumite? Where is the connection?"

Kata interpretation worldwide has been gradually morphing into more sophisticated bunkai better approximating the exact movements of a form. This was particularly noticeable after the rise of Gracie-introduced MMA/jujitsu matches. Hopefully, these revelations may revive the kata arts currently ebbing in the U.S.

Author Nathan Johnson in his excellent book *Barefoot Zen* remarked that if you are looking for a rationale in kata, you generally will not find one. He took the early opinion that no substantial logic or strategy existed within these forms. However, once we introduce kata's missing Kiko principles you will see an intelligent and sophisticated methodology emerge for how to engage a hostile body. Solutions to a wide range of common attacks will appear.

In my early studies as a *kyudansha* (pre black belt) kata did seem like a bunch of random, but cool techniques. However, this was not my experience in my later years of advanced study. As I delved

169

in the essential nature of the Isshinryu forms, I found ever more credible rationales and consistencies. All the major kata consist of movement sets that address an attack from start to finish. They all teach the fundamental techniques of control and neutralization.

The purpose of kata is not to introduce fragmented, choreographed self-defense techniques, but to build upon a central theme of common responses to the keenly observed nature of physical hostilities.

CHALLENGE 39

The slip-step can be initiated with either a front or rear foot. It's all the same action. Move forward in a stable fashion without having one foot cross another.

REBELLION

A slip step is any action taken by the legs in which one foot initiates movement forward or backward but does not cross the other leg. A slip step can move to any point on the compass; front, back, sides. A common or forward slip step is when the foot closest to the direction you intend to move initiates the action followed by the foot furthest from that direction moving in kind. A certain proportionately in width and length should be followed. The most favorable proportion is a one-foot length step forward. That is, the length of your own foot.

A 'step,' by contrast, can be defined as one foot crossing in front of or behind another for the purpose of changing position or location.

It is true that you will end up in the same position after slip-stepping forward with either a right or left foot initiating. But each action causes a different energetic outcome. Slipping with a left foot lead increases left arm strength if the hand is closed. Slipping with a right foot lead increases arm strength if the hand is open. The length and width of a slip-step will directly affect the body energy, which will in turn affect the strength of a desired action. Incorrect slip-stepping will work against you.

There are two ways to slip-step forward. You can initiate with the lead foot or the rear foot. In considering proportionality, wider steps versus narrower steps will yield different energetic outcomes. Yes! It makes a big difference in strength if you change the proportionality of your step.

CHALLENGE 40

The karate obi is worn to hold up your gi

pants and to display your rank.

REBELLION

These two reasons only define the obi's functional and symbolic purpose.

There is another explanation, rarely discussed. The obi has an Esoteric/Internal rationale. A karate belt should be worn loosely around the waist because pressure on the abdomen from an overly tight belt restricts Ki flow. The knot of the obi is to be worn directly over the lower dantien (the physical seat of power) to focus subliminal attention on the *hara*, the body's electro-magnetic reservoir. By 'subliminal,' I mean that you don't have to hold your conscious attention on your hara with your belt knot worn there. Your mind will be passively aware of the knot.

The belt tabs are also to be worn hanging evenly and proportionately down the inside of the thighs. This position allows Yin energy to better rise up from the inside of the legs into the dantien. The actual belt, providing it's constructed from natural materials (cotton/silk), will act as a conduit or facilitator for this energy flow. As strange as it may sound, your belt tabs can amplify your Ki flow.

It is unfortunate, but understandable, that modern obi are being manufactured with increasingly more synthetic materials. To keep costs down martial manufacturers are substituting plastics that negatively affect the human biofield. Whenever possible, purchase a 100% cotton, naturally-dyed belt. Natural fibers and materials are in sync with the physical body's energy fields and facilitate a better flow of Ki.

CHALLENGE 41

Karate belt colors display rank classifications.

REBELLION

Rank display is not the only function the karate belt colors convey.

Each color stimulates a *chakra* or energy center within the body. The word *Chakra* (wheel) is a yogic Hindu observation that recognizes the body as containing seven distinct energy centers found along the spine that correspond to the seven major glands. Each chakra generates a specific color frequency, which in turn activates specific musculature.

Colors vibrate at different frequencies. Even though the obi is worn on the outside of the gi, its color vibration influences meridian flow, which in turn influences physical strength. The ideal belt color sequence would follow the color spectrum; red, orange, yellow, green, indigo, blue and violet, the corresponding chakric frequencies. It's interesting how close martial belt colors actually come to matching this color spectrum. Hence, the Karate obi serves as a subliminal frequency modulator.

The typical reaction I get to statements like this are rolled eyeballs followed by, 'How can inanimate objects have any effect on physical strength?' They can and they do. This was known by advanced practitioners within the monastic martial community. This is a lost art today with only a few revivalists attempting to restore these teachings.

Welcome to the 21st century. Quantum Physics is letting us know that it's time to recognize that all objects are in essence, energetic events with their own unique cause and effect.

CHALLENGE 42

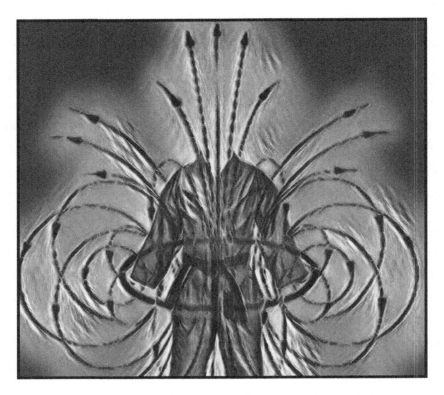

The karate gi is a more functional martial garb for training than a t-shirt or sweatshirt. It was designed to give practitioners greater freedom of movement and to take abuse.

REBELLION

The karate gi may not give us insight into how to fight in modern clothing but it does give us insight into clothing's overall effect upon the Human Subtle Energy field.

Like the obi, there is an esoteric rationale behind the wearing of the karate gi. The gi jacket, by extending below the waist, helps to contain energy in the torso's energy reservoir, the lower dantien.

Dantians

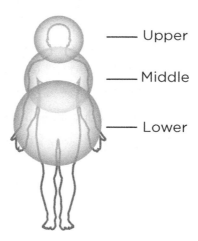

—— Upper

—— Middle

—— Lower

By contrast, Western wear, which has men's shirts often tucked into their pants and a belt cinched around the waist, splits the dantien. And so, our outer wear reveals something of our inner energy orientation. This clothing split causes more energy to be held in the upper body. This is partly why Western cultures are so heady.

We also get a clue to the nature of karate training itself by looking closely at our training garb. If karate only stressed ballistic blocks/

strikes, we would not need to justify a karate-style gi, since nothing would ever be grabbed. Wearing a t-shirt would be just as effective as a thick cotton jacket. The karate uniform suggests that grabbing/grappling was a prominent part of training. Yet, with the exportation of martial arts into the United States, beginning in the mid to late 1960's, we saw very little grappling within traditional Okinawan and Japanese arts outside of judo and jujitsu. A clear segregation between the grappling and striking systems existed.

As to color, why wear white? And why is the gi jacket crossed left over right? White is a 'metal' color, associated with the lungs of the body and the direction West, according to the Japanese Five Element practitioners. Obviously, undyed/unbleached cloth is cheaper than dyed cloth, and karate gis get a lot of wear and tear. The early gi's in the U.S. tended to be unbleached, tan colored uniforms. Of course, a gi is a great way to advertise your discipline. That notion aside, the Esoteric Teachings reveal that the left over right fold is in sync with the body's rotational energy field. Upon death Japanese bodies are wrapped with the fold right over left, an acknowledgement that the life spirit has left the deceased.

CHALLENGE 43

Fight, Fight, Fight!

Karate is all about the fight.

REBELLION

You don't need to train for years, certainly not decades, to be able to defend yourself. And if you love fighting, you are probably winning more bouts than loosing. Kumite in any serious form takes a heavy toll on the joints, bones, and soft tissue. It generates far too many injuries, and the general stress of actual combat is bad for the body. I've spoken with dojo students who tell me they "fight" every class. But I doubt their idea of fighting would be recognized as such by the old world masters. What we deem in the Traditional dojo as 'fighting' is a watered down version compared to the harshness of ancient practices where life and death were real everyday concerns. Fighting simply grinds down the body and saps one of energy to get up and work the next day. Of course, there are plenty of adrenaline junkies who need their next fight fix. In truth, most karate students are actually trying to avoid a fight, unless you are a committed competitor.

There are many great benefits to martial arts training beyond fighting; the therapeutic; keeping your body fit and your mind alert. The meditative; developing your spiritual sensitivity. Martial monastics took their arts to great heights of self-expression by incorporating the practical with the healing and meditative aspects into their daily practices. This later dimension enabled the Japanese samurai to make sense of their violent world and find a way to live fully in the present moment.

In America we have taken the concept of the fight to be all-important, but the wider possibilities mentioned above can yield many more immediate and relevant day-to-day benefits.

CHALLENGE 44

Karate, karate-jutsu, karate-do are all

names for the same underlying art.

REBELLION

Though they may be viewed as the same labels by modern standards, there is a world of difference between karate, karate jutsu, and karate-dō practice.

Chinese martial arts of Buddhist influence were referred to as *Quan* or *Chuan Fa*, literally, Clasped Hand Dharma (the fist clutches the Buddha's teachings). The Japanese called the Chuan Fa arts, Kempo. Later, the Okinawans placed their Chinese-influenced arts under the general label, *Kara-te*, a mix of Chinese influence with their indigenous island fighting techniques. When the spiritual element was present, the art was called, karate-dō. Karate's history owes a great deal to the influences of its ancestral Chinese arts. But Chinese monastic traditions based their fighting arts upon even older, Indian Buddhist *Vajramukti* teachings of non-violent self-defense, healing, health-nourishing, and spiritual discipline. The temple monastic sought to transcend conflict altogether by using the martial arts as a ladder of ritual practices and experiences to this end. Whenever you come across the terms, *karate, karate-dō, or kempo*, keep in mind that their modern context often deviates greatly from their ancient one. Many of today's martial arts proponents no longer ally themselves to any formal spiritual practices.

The *Dō* (Chinese, *Tao*) is an Asian philosophical concept that emerged from deep introspection and generations-long ascetic practices and inquiries. The concept of the Dō or 'Way' dates back into China's mythical antiquity. The Japanese term '*Dō*' and its Chinese predecessor, '*Tao*,' describes a Way of Being. This Way of Being is cultivated through spiritual or ritual practice—meditation being one of the primary methods. Ritual practice aims at aligning oneself with the naturally flowing action of our universe. Professor Malcolm David Eckle of Boston University believes that ritual practice formed a "mezzocosm," a middle path, or bridge linking one's inside (micro) and outside (macro) worlds. The Dō also defines a way of life influenced by disciplined self-study, one valuing spiritual existence alongside and in balance with material existence. At its core, the Dō of martial arts aims to dissolve conflict absolutely in the same way that the external martial arts seek to vanquish a physical enemy.

CHALLENGE 45

We all know how to perform perfect Isshinryu kata because we have concise archival video footage of Shimabuku and his successors.

REBELLION

Despite historically significant video records of Shimabuku's kata, Isshinryu forms are actually incredibly nuanced. And no video can ever capture the internal dynamics of a form. Subtle technicalities, which include specific visualizations and other mental foci along with precise breathing patterns are not visible to the naked eye. In fact, this depth of teaching was rarely made available outside of monastic settings. In addition, both Ungi Uezu and Kichiro Shimabuku, who took the reigns of the system on Okinawa after Shimabuku's passing, do not perform their Isshin kata with the same emphasis as its founder. All we can glean from their performances, which show subtle changes from the founder, is the outer shell of their art. We have no idea of the system's inner structure without explanation from knowledgeable Isshinryu masters who understand their art's Esoteric nature. These teachers are few and far between.

CHALLENGE 46

The interior design of a dojo and your

personal training area has little effect

upon your martial development, strength

or performance.

REBELLION

Chinese geomantic, *Feng Shui* masters would heartily disagree.

Feng Shui is the art of understanding and manipulating the energy of objects and the space containing them by specific arrangement. From the Esoteric standpoint, the space we choose to train in, and the objects we bring into our training space, are equally as important as the bodies we inhabit. A proper training area can uplift, stimulate, advance, even heighten the training experience. Esoteric masters configured their training areas with an understanding of energy flow to create the optimal conditions within their immediate environment.

A good training area should be clutter free, have the mouth of Ki (entrance to the dojo), unblocked. The dojo should be tidy, clean, sunny, if possible, and follow Feng Shui's Five Element Phases of having appropriate sections of the dojo in balance. One can start to appreciate any dojo's interior organization by asking how you feel in the space. Does it feel light and airy, heavy or dense, hot or cold, open or closed, uplifting, inviting or restricting?

Just as one attends to the slightest detail of his or her kata, the same exactitude should go into the selection of the training space, the objects and their placement within it. This level of detail will elevate any dojo to one of sacred or ritual space and invite the Dō or Spirit into the training experience.

CHALLENGE 47

Ki (Chi) does not exist!

REBELLION

There are bio-mechanistic-oriented martial artists today who firmly believe that no such intrinsic 'energy' as Ki exists. Of course, this would erase 3,000 years of Ki's recognition and history in China, the basis of Traditional Chinese and Indian Medicine, acupuncture, a significant portion of Yogic Culture, the monastic martial sciences, metaphysics, and we might as well throw in Quantum Physic's scientific insights into the hidden world of matter on the quantum level.

The skeptics rely on the fact that since no science has uncovered the mystery of Ki to date it must not exist. But new technologies and new theories are emerging every year to help us penetrate these intriguing mysteries.

What the skeptics overlook is that the Indian and Chinese cultures meticulously mapped out the behavior of this unknown energy in their martial arts and embedded its principles into their movement forms.

Of the thousands of experiments conducted by my organization alone over a twenty-five year testing period there were hundreds of strength outcomes unexplainable by either body biomechanics or self-suggestion.

Our philosophy is to encourage students interested in this subject to work with a knowledgeable Internal Isshinryu teacher who can guide you to experience the phenomenon of Ki for yourself.

CHALLENGE 48

Martial art training is a *physical* discipline.

If a sensei wants to impart psychology,

let him get certified as a

therapist, motivational, or Life coach.

REBELLION

Isshinryu can offer one a whole person training if you know where to look.

At the heyday of martial arts in China, the Chuan Fa or Kempo arts were looked at philosophically, cosmologically, therapeutically, practically, and spiritually. Teachers were revered as warriors, healers/priests and monks. The arts were far more holistic in their training perspectives. The arrival of World War II changed the momentum of the Okinawan and Japanese martial arts. Masters died during the war and many of their potential successors shucked the rigors of the fighting arts to make money in the booming Industrial Revolution.

Mao's Cultural Revolution in China (1966-1976) drastically altered the direction and purpose of the Chinese martial arts. Teachers were pressured to emphasize the therapeutic and minimize the combative side of training. Also, as some of these complex disciplines moved into the future, they began to fragment. Teachings became compartmentalized much like the U.S. medical profession's splintering into Medical specialties. People simply did not have the free time to spend years upon years of complex and rigorous study. Today, some sensei inadvertently further reduce their systems to simple fitness, self-defense or sport instruction to enhance their dojo's profitability. All these factors have diluted a once highly concentrated process of evolving one physically, mentally, emotionally and spiritually. The techniques of Isshinryu themselves grew out of older, martial monastic traditions that emphasized building character and exploring mindfulness in a multi-dimensional fashion.

If modern martial arts swing too far over to the superficial side of training, while excluding the other great attributes of study, we will lose valuable knowledge that was once part of martial legacy for thousands of years in Asia.

Today's sensei have to be more versatile and sensitive to the changing needs of the culture. The teaching environment has become more challenging with children now making up the bulk of practitioners.

An awakened sensei has far more responsibility than simply teaching kicks and punches. As teachers, we are all life coaches and mentors, and therefore have a responsibility to be as mentally clear as we are physically sharp. Among our many unspoken tasks; we have to avoid or diffuse the cheap shots, mind traps and ego wars. We have to keep the mad dogs at bay, which may require sometimes pulling the angry, soul-wounded off their victims. We may have to lay down a fairness law with a compassionate foot or fist, and avoid exploiting others due to our station as mentors. We have to craft our message to be understood by mixed age levels and intelligences. We have to lean into the strong winds of superficiality without breaking our own passion or our student's desire to learn. We have to juggle multiple teaching paces and techniques to keep students' interests alive. We have to take a dynamic mosaic of psyches and create a balanced collage of energies, all pulling for the same shore. We have to revitalize the weak, realign the dispirited, and awaken bodies, sometimes in minutely small time frames. We may have to honor what has never been honored, give back what we never stole, and remain detached from the outcomes. We have to watch our own bodies age in the candid mirror of the youths before us. We have to be the wise elders in a world of ever-scarce wisdom. We have to hold out our promises on the value of our disciplines and on the merit of our souls. We have to keep hammering and shaping the living blades, no matter how superior or inferior the steel.

Every sensei worth his or her salt in the dojo cares about his art, the process and the students that support him. Every sensei that teaches with compassion enables the flame of his martial art to burn brighter into the future.

CHALLENGE 49

There are no more secrets in the martial

arts. We have access to any and all

information needed to advance to a

high degree of skill, thanks to the

World Wide Web

REBELLION

We have such an abundance of martial information at our fingertips today, more than anyone could ever process in a lifetime. However, there still exists information mostly lost, buried, or forgotten that can be found in small, private martial circles. These closely held insights and techniques can contribute greatly to the future advance of the martial arts.

Much of the commonly available information is redundant. Many teachers of a particular style, for example, often demonstrate the same material on Youtube. We are top heavy with demonstration, light on explanation.

Within the Isshinryu community alone we have hundreds of teachers exhibiting the same kata, each showing his or her prowess at duplicating the master's forms. We need more detailed explanation for why these particular forms were created and the exact lessons they were imparting.

There is a vast tier of little known Esoteric practices embedded within Isshinryu that we are on the verge of accessing today. The following story illustrates an example of hidden technique.

I was showing an adult class an escape from a front choke. I observed that the majority of the class was not paying attention to the details of the release. So, to make a point, I demonstrated an advanced internal concept that stressed the importance of this detail. I stated that I would share this technique but reserve the explanation for more advanced students. Everyone noted how seemingly effortless the small shift in his detail effected their escape.

One ten-year disciple wanted the explanation. So he sought the answer from a senior *sempai*, who refused to comment. This brown belt then reached out to other yudansha (black belts). No one spoke. This only egged him on. He vowed to me that he would discover the answer by searching on Google. "Fine," I replied. The student did not find the answer on Google. During the course of a year, this brown belt's curiosity was so great he offered the head instructor of another dojo, *"the price of one private lesson,"* if he could solve the mystery of this particular escape. That sensei could not figure out why the technique worked so well.

Months later, a former Tae Kwon Do champion happened to drop by my class. By coincidence he was also shown the same technique without the explanation for why it worked so well. With great curiosity, he too went on his own search for an answer. He eventually found an instructor who bluntly told him, "Pressure Points." When he confidently returned to me with this answer, I asked, *"Which* pressure points?" The Tae Kwon do expert did not know. "The answer is not pressure points. Keep digging," I replied. There was one more senior teacher, someone with decades of experience that he would ask. Three months later, he returned to my dojo and revealed that senior teacher's answer, "Honestly, I don't have the faintest idea!"

Not everything is available in Google Search. There are subtle levels of martial techniques still closely guarded by their adherents. After nearly five decades of study, I can state confidently, no one has seen it all.

CHALLENGE 50

Isshinryu's future depends

upon its practitioners doing the same.

REBELLION

To flourish, Isshinryu must adapt to every culture's changing needs. Traditional martial arts are waning in the U.S. Kata is still not well understood or broadly embraced. Kata, although intriguing, was originally introduced into this country with too much ambiguity and mystique. This resulted in less people interested in pursuing them and taking the time to understand their true depth.

Young children and young adults now make up the bulk of martial practitioners in America. This cohort is reshaping the martial arts. Many of today's youth find kata training too demanding, particularly in a society that gives them little time to attend to serious practice. Training time has been decreasing amongst the average martial student since the early 1970's. I suspect we will find a quickening of this degeneration to a correlation of our access to the World Wide Web in the 1990's with our ever-increasing marriages to our digital devices.

In the 1950's, Gichin Funakoshi modified the Okinawan kata when he went to Japan. He felt the kata were too complicated for the average Japanese. His actions seem to foreshadow the same problems the Traditional martial arts now face in the United States.

CHALLENGE 51

Isshinryu karate and martial arts in general have little in common with yoga.

REBELLION

Holistic martial training is a complete form of Yoga.

The difference in training goals can be found in your endgame for practice. From a monastic viewpoint, Kata is a Yogic discipline embodied within the philosophical and physical structure of scientific martial principles. Many students are unaware that the Indians called *Chi Kung*, Yoga. Karate Dō could therefore be defined as Yoga at its finest and possibly one of the most calculated forms of Yoga the Ancients ever devised. *Tensho, Seisan,* and *Sanchin* Kata are some of the oldest Buddhist movement patterns (also referred to as mandalas) developed in China.

Indian Yogis and Chinese Kempo masters long ago also recognized the link between physical movement and consciousness. The latter group elected to use natural body movement patterns rather than exaggerated physical postures to reach the same evolutionary goals; heightened sensitivity, powerful practical skills, healing patterns and radical shifts in consciousness toward a more fulfilling life.

CHALLENGE 52

The basic I or H pattern that Shimabuku

once taught is seldom practiced today

because it is not necessary to the system.

REBELLION

Shimabuku once taught a short form akin to the Japanese *Taikyo-ku* (First Cause) or early *Heian* Forms, often referred to as the I or H patterns. This pattern likely derived from his Shorinryu training. The routine gradually disappeared from Isshinryu's base curriculum. But this basic form is more revealing then one might expect. Some very old Esoteric Teachings were encoded in its innocuous block/punch routine, unknown by modern sensei.

This encoding may also be linked to one of the oldest Asian symbols, the Buddhist *Svastika*. The origins of the Svastika date back nearly 11,000 years well before it was appropriated and maligned by Germany's Nazi regime.

When this symbol is broken apart into its North/South and East/West ⌐, you have the actual diagram of the I Form pattern. The I Form looks like a capital letter 'I' *conceptually*, that is, in your mind's eye. Walking the pattern reveals that the *actual* floor diagram is one arm of the Svastika.

This is important to note because some Esoteric Forms are only properly activated when facing compass North. Even more interesting is that the East/West arm is the only other activation direction to perform the set correctly. The goal in this preferred directional execution was to preserve vital Kiko principles of how the human body interacts with the Earth's geomagnetic, lunar and solar fields. In this simple structure, we clearly see a unique martial yoga unfolding through natural, calculated movement patterns in harmony with the external energy fields that envelop us.

Both the left and right sides of the body, and the North versus South facing compass directions during the performance, condition the performer to maximize energy flow through the limbs. The postures, although appearing as simple block/strike sequences, were nuanced in cadence, limb action, and breath control. Mirrored configurations were not only slightly different from left to right sides but reversed when facing south. The breathing and sound of the exhalation changed in tone and pitch to enhance proper meridian flow as one moved through the low, middle and high blocking motions.

This form appears unassuming but it contains a trove of information about old world tactical and energetic rationales to unleash tremendous power. Isshinryu teachers should reconsider bringing it back into their curriculums.

The General Pathway of Ki Flow

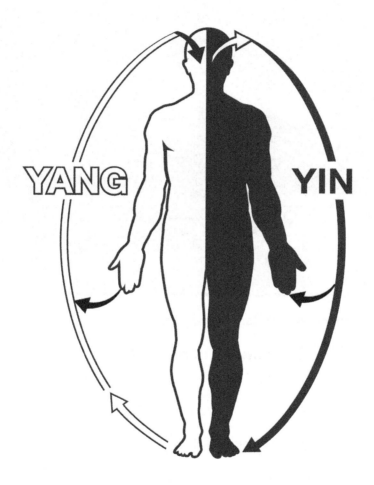

CHALLENGE 53

Isshinryu sensei have a firm grasp on the entirety of their art.

REBELLION

The techniques that comprise Isshinryu were gathered from a lengthy history of martial arts extending over several thousand years, stretching back to the warrior class called the *Kashatrya* in India.

Tatsuo Shimabuku did not create Okinawan karate. He learned karate and its kata from his predecessors. He further selected and modified these patterns to what he felt were the best techniques for himself and his fledgling system. Within this broader legacy of technique we have discovered a wealth of martial information far in excess of what Shimabuku collected and taught. Few Isshinryu teachers have seen, been exposed to, or been taught the Esoteric/Internal components that were embedded into the fundamental patterns that make up the Isshin art long before Shimabuku himself was exposed to karate. It's not for anyone's lack of curiosity or passion that these elements are overlooked.

Let's change this.

CHALLENGE 54

Neihanchi kata is a fighting form to be

used when your back is up against a wall,

on a narrow bridge, or in a corridor.

REBELLION

Is this description of Neihanchi's purpose realistic for modern society?

Was this the actual purpose for this form's pattern? How many fights might this entail? Rebel Isshinryu reveals that Neihanchi's aim might instead be teaching one how to use an opponent as a wall or shield to *narrow* the attacking corridor, and as a means of shielding yourself from multiple attacks.

Historically, Neihanchi was a Chi Kung, inner-cultivating, grappling kata, one of three framework forms that explored the full range of upper limb seizing, locking and escaping possibilities. This kata taught multiple grip styles, numerous arm and wrist-locks, and how to organize the body's energy system to maximize the rotational or torque strength of the torso.

Neihanchi contains intriguing hidden nuances and a unique hand formation, called the Motobu Fist. This fist is often mistakenly considered a punch when it is used primarily to enhance the torso's rotational power.

213

CHALLENGE 55

Sanchin kata is a Hard style or

External form.

REBELLION

The statement that Sanchin kata is considered the 'be all and end all' form is rarely explained in detail.

In the Esoteric tradition, Sanchin is performed as a Soft, Internal or *Kokyu* form.

Aston Hugh is a long-term Okinawan karate veteran and healer with sixty years of martial experience. In addition to his advanced study of Isshinryu, he extended his studies into Gojuryu, T'ai Chi Ch'uan and the *Liu He Ba Fa* (Water Boxing method). Hugh shared with me his observations how too many Hard stylists would often damage their bodies with extreme training methods and some-times, unnecessary physical tension. Hugh believes that Sanchin kata was actually created as a Soft style form to be done com-pletely relaxed. According to Hugh, all the shaking and trembling we see in a proper Sanchin performance is the result of a large volume of Ki being released through the body, causing it to sway, shake or vibrate. This 'trembling' phenomenon is referred to as 'Induced Ki flow'.

In the Esoteric Teachings there is also a pre-Sanchin preparation and a post-Sanchin release rarely, if ever, discussed.

CHALLENGE 56

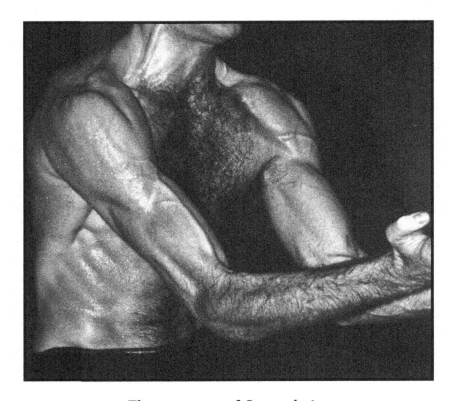

The purpose of Sunsu kata,

with its similar movements to other

Isshinryu forms, is clear to most sensei.

REBELLION

There is scant information available regarding Sunsu kata's technical depth or its odd similarity to moves found in the Seisan, Wansu and Sanchin forms. And we have little direct commentary from Shimabuku on the subject.

However, a few theories might be helpful to broaden the dialog about this kata.

One of the oldest known variations of Sanchin is credited to the Uechiryu style. Uechiryu Sanchin gives a clue to why Shimabuku may have created Sunsu. On careful analysis, Sunsu appears to be a Yin form, more closely following the Uechi-style with the left foot forward, first step. Tatsuo's Sanchin is a Yang form, noted by the kata starting with a right foot forward. The two kata distinguish themselves with slight variations in the way the arm motions are executed in the opening sequence. It's possible that successive Isshinryu teachers may not have noticed this distinction and may have inadvertently standardized the sequence. One theory is that Shimabuku may have introduced Sunsu as his way of emphasizing Yin motions to compliment all the other Yang-styled kata in his Form syllabus. Sunsu's opening sequence may also have been Shimabuku's attempt to show students how to apply Sanchin combatively.

This also suggests a different interpretation for the kata's name as 'Strong man'. This could be an indirect reference to Internal power, usually cultivated by the more advanced student, or achieved by the time someone has reached older age.

As to the Form's reference of being composed in part with pieces of previous kata, only at quick glance does this appear to be true. In reality, these sequences are reversed. This is significant. In the Esoteric Teachings a reversal implies a change in energy polarity where a Yang move becomes a Yin move and vice versa. Yin and Yang moves are performed with different breathing patterns, cadences and nuances to the techniques. The Wansu dumping throw, for example, is reversed in Sunsu. Also the elbow series moving right/left/left is opposite of Seisan's punch/punch/kick/punch motions that move left/right/left. We believe that Shimabuku's Sunsu kata was demonstrating how to activate Esoteric Principles when doing sequences on the reverse side from the other fighting forms.

CHALLENGE 57

Everything that Tatsuo taught represents

the totality of Isshinryu.

REBELLION

Isshinryu was a work-in-progress for Tatsuo Shimabuku up to his death in 1975. The system remains a work-in-progress for modern Isshinryu sensei. Shimabuku's open-minded, rebellious and exploratory mindset has encouraged professionals around the world to continue searching for more answers and relevancy. With the creation of Isshinryu, Tatsuo Shimabuku has provided an excellent platform, a solid starting point, for its hierarchy to advance his creation.

However, there is much more that can be gained and to learn by embracing the Esoteric Tradition's internal, therapeutic, meditative and spiritual realms. These principles can offer further enhancements to round out Isshinryu as a practical fighting system. One of the oldest spiritual works from the great Indian sages offers us some clear and simple advice;

Wake up! Don't be lazy.
Follow the right path,
avoid the wrong.
You will be happy here
as well as hereafter.

Dhammapada

Translation by Eknath Easwaran

Isshinryu Karate:
From The Outside Looking In
Interview with Shifu Hayashi

What qualifies you to comment on Isshinryu and Okinawan karate in general?

I began formal karate study in 1968 in Isshin Shorin Ji Ryu Okinawan Te under Sensei Robert Murphy (1937-2007) at the pioneering Bank Street Dojo (1962-1984) in Summit NJ. Murphy's system was a combination of Isshin and Shorinryu, formed when Isshinryu's founder, Tatsuo Shimabuku, was still experimenting and making modifications to his own technical Shorinryu base. Murphy's hybrid system retained many of Shimabuku's former Shorin influences. Murphy was also a senior student of, and senior instructor for, the New Jersey master, Don Nagle (1938-1999). Murphy was a familiar and respected teacher at Nagle's Dojo, and well-steeped in Isshinryu tradition. As many Northeast-based, Isshinryu practitioners know, Don Nagle was a highly regarded, first generation, American Isshinryu master, awarded 10th dan on October 17, 1987 in Knoxville, Tennessee by Tatsuo Shimabuku. Along with Lewis Lizzotte and Harold Long these three men were the earliest, highest ranked black belts in Isshinryu in the U.S. Nagle was instrumental in the propagation of Isshinryu in New Jersey and is appropriately considered 'Father of Isshinryu' in this state. Although I am the successor of a style called Isshin Kempo, an offshoot that evolved out of Murphy's and sensei William Scott

223

Russell's influences, my training has essentially remained committed to the isshin blueprint. I hold dan ranking in Isshinryu proper as well. Most importantly, I have practiced the eight kata of Tatsuo Shimabuku's Isshinryu system for forty-eight years. I am also a career martial arts teacher. Not only have I diligently practiced these forms myself. I have taught them to thousands of individuals, many of who asked intelligent questions and shared their commentary about their personal experiences practicing these kata.

The reason I teach Isshin Kempo is not due to any lack of credibility in Tatsuo's Isshinryu karate, but rather due to the emphasis my former teacher, William Scott Russell (Author of *Karate The Energy Connection,* Delacorte Press, 1976) placed on our training. Russell, a controversial figure for his radical ideas, suggested that Isshinryu may have been under-interpreted by the first generation mainstream Isshinryu community. He didn't say, "misinterpreted." By under-interpreted, he meant that other layers of technical depth within the Isshin kata system were not being discussed, practiced, or exhibited. Evidence of this unspoken technical knowledge and its relevancy to the art eventually became too obvious for me to deny.

In my early study as a young, twenty-year old *kyudansha* (colored belt holder) under Russell's tutelage, I lacked enough comparative insights to validate or challenge his perspective. But now, nearly five decades later, I agree with his initial observation. My organization's position on this matter makes Isshin Kempo something of a rebel Isshinryu karate system. We consider ourselves to be Isshinryu's *internal* sister art. Of course, we are not the first or only group to splinter from mainstream or orthodox Isshinryu with ideas falling outside the traditional Isshinryu box. We see clear evidence of alterations in the texture of performance within Shimabuku's own Okinawan bloodline, in Ungi Uezu's and Kichiro Shimabuku's exhibitions. Both men express their Isshinryu differently in both spirit and mechanical performances from the founder. Our rebellion is not directed toward the founder, his martial offspring, or any other Isshinryu teacher or hierarchy, or what Isshinryu practitioners have come to validate and teach in their personal study of Isshinryu karate. Ours is a rebellion against what we saw in the early 1970's as an over-simplified, over-stylized, misunderstood, but certainly commercially viable Okinawan civilian defense art. This was the result of not fully matured martial art teachers. We were a naive Western culture when it came to our comprehension of Asian martial culture. We took a very rich discipline and played superficially with its components. We believed then, and continue to believe now with more certainty, that Isshinryu itself is a continuing thread of a many thousand's year martial legacy in possession of far more depth and dimensionality than is currently being espoused by its American orthodox hierarchy. Though we do not share the same basics and have additional non-isshin forms and other technical information in our system, we do share Shimabuku's entire kata syllabi. However, our interpretative perspective dramatically differs from the conventional one. As a tight knit, five decades long martial organization, we are intrigued with Isshinryu's links to earlier, older and broader systems – particularly the Shaolin (Shorin), Buddhist, and *Naha te* lineages that ran through Okinawan history. These lineages formed the basis for much of Shimabuku's technical legacy. Our studies have penetrated into a much deeper layer of lessons than the mainstream promotes, particularly in regard to Isshinryu kata *bunkai* (applications). This is due to the influences of Kiko principles uncovered over the last twenty-five years of my study. Noting some of these differences and distinctions without using the Kiko label, Russell felt it more appropriate to call his system Isshin Kempo. Kempo was an early term for karate and the Japanese term for Chinese *Quan fa*. Readers should consider that Isshin Kempo is an extension of Tatsuo's Isshinryu house, similar to those who believe that Isshinryu was an extension of Shimabuku's Shorin art. The 'kempo' additive describes and defines our affiliation to an older, more comprehensive Shaolin system that embraces not just combative, but healing and meditative dimensions of training.

Barring the therapeutic and meditative components for a moment, if we focus solely on the combative sphere, we find a well-crafted diversity of standing grappling technique and perhaps, more importantly, *aiki* or *bioenergetic* principles alongside the commonly taught ballistic techniques of the system. We do not need to look outside into other arts to find *aiki* principles in Isshinryu. These principles are inherent in the Isshin forms themselves.

We both hold to the observation and teach that Sanchin kata was and is a very rich Chi-Kung or Kiko exercise whose primary purpose was and is to develop internal strength in a logical, coherent way. Contrary to what you may read about in the popular literature about this kata, its central purpose was to primarily exercise what we in the West call the Auric, Subtle Energy Body, or Biofield, not *just* the physical body. These terms, *Subtle Energy Body* or *Biofield* were non-existent in ancient Asian martial practices, or Okinawan martial nomenclature.

If I lose readers who find themselves with no concept of what I am referring to or hold on to a limited perspective that no such thing as KI, or an 'Energy Body' exists, I'd like to share a quick story illustrating some general reactions I've received to my statement. A few years ago I got a phone call from a high-dan ranked Okinawan stylist who had read an article I had published in 2001 in the former *Journal of Asian Martial Arts* (JAMA). He asked if I would be interested in talking with him about Internal Energy. He went on to explain that everyone he had approached within the Hard style community either did not know about the subject, spoke about it in broad strokes, or did not want to talk about it. He was genuinely surprised when I obliged him. Some time later, he met an Aikido sensei and queried him about the existence of 'Ki' principles in his art. The Aikido sensei gave a vague explanation. When the Texas Yamashita karate expert commented how the position of the feet in various stances effected Ki distribution in the body, the Aikido sensei simply fell mute. He had nothing to add. "It was as if I was speaking German," the karate expert said.

Most American martial artists, particularly in the Hard style disciplines, even many in the Soft style arts, understand internal energy work either in broad terms or only in an intuitive, non-verbal, closed-mouth cultural manner. When it comes to specifics, the martial community often muddles for words or gropes for specific examples. Rebel Isshinryu has developed an articulate and concise language to advance the specifics of internal work as it relates to basic technique in all types of fighting arts and, in particular, to the Isshinryu kata. Our principles have been proven over and again with men and women of all ages, from different styles, over a twenty-five year research period. One might chose to call these events by a different label but the central point is that Kiko is present in the art of Isshinryu and when applied correctly, it works dramatically well.

Okinawans referred to Chi Kung as *Kiko or Kokyu,* and the Shorin system from which Shimabuku gained notoriety as a master is replete with extensive internal training methods, concepts, principles and techniques. This knowledge has not spilled over to the Isshinryu world at large in any clear and cohesive way. This is not anyone's fault, nor should its lack in Isshinryu's curriculum be considered premeditated. Americans simply were not aware of Subtle Energy principles in their martial arts. I also do not believe that the Okinawan masters were all too keen on imparting them to their post World War II conquerors. Even if they did, there was a formidable missing bridge of language to convey the complexity of the subject.

Just as U.S. food manufacturers have stripped the essential nutrients from most of our food grains, we too have inadvertently, perhaps due to our Western orientation, stripped some essential teachings and principles from our Traditional martial art forms. We think its time to put this tiger back into the Isshinryu tank, and reinsert these dormant principles back into the forms. We want to reinvigorate the Hard arts by revealing their hidden soft skill set.

Much of the mythology surrounding Isshinryu that I discuss in this work has to do with Okinawan karate's missing link to its internal face.

What do you see in the Isshin kata and the way you practice them that differs significantly from mainstream Isshinryu and the way you used to practice them?

I don't question the Isshinryu system as a practical, efficient, personal civil defense system. I hold Tatsuo Shimabuku's creation in high regard. His martial teachings are the bread and butter for all my current studies. My statements are not an attempt to undermine the benefits or the value of what other Isshinryu teachers offer their followers. It's hard to even pin down what advanced mainstream Isshinryu is today because so many teachers add their own nuances. Certainly, Isshinryu's spread into the United States gives us a unique presentation from the perspective of the early Okinawan karate masters, Tatuso being the primary one, followed by Ungi Uezu, Kichiro and their senior American counterparts, who added their own spin to the style. Some first generation American experts had initially obtained higher ranking than Tatsuo's son, Kichiro and his son-in-law, Ungi Uezu. According to James Advincula, "They (first generation) didn't know what they had." We have found an extraordinary depth, for example, in standing grappling techniques inherent in the Isshin kata that were not presented in the early 1970's. More remarkably, we've found a comprehensive Kiko or internal infrastructure that rivals, at least in theory, if not in principle, the great Chinese internal arts of Tai Chi, Ba Gua and Hsing Yi. Where these latter arts might speak openly about such principles, the karate disciplines have maintained a history of covert, concealed language and in the worst cases, offer its disciples an empty cup where such principles are simply absent or not carried forward.

Isshinryu's American pioneers were taught the outer form, the externals of their art; speed, power, balance, coordination etc. and their lethal practicality. Consider that Western culture had never witnessed anything like the Asian fighting arts until around the 1950's. There is little evidence that knowledge of the vibratory frequencies, Subtle Energy body, Pranic or extensive Kiko principles were ever taught *en masse* from the early 1950'-70's and particularly to Americans in the late 1950's through 1990's. It was only with the advent of the televised MMA and jujitsu matches from the front-running promoters like the Gracie jujitsu family that we saw a shift in traditional martial thinking away from exclusively ballistic technique. The standing kick/punch fighters who engaged the jujitsu masters failed miserably to assert their control via striking. They had to accept both the reality and the value of ground fighting and adapt their styles appropriately to ground tactics. Many Karate sensei's hands were forced to either improve their defense for being taken down, and/or learn how to ground fight, which meant either refining or adding a new tier of technique to their kick/punch curriculums or find themselves isolated from an emerging, younger male community both intrigued and hungry for this definitive skill set. I say definitive, because we, in the striking arts, know fully well that there is no guarantee if you strike someone they are going to go down. On the other hand, if you place someone in a wristlock and arm bar, you know pretty sure they are in trouble. Even if an adversary should escape these locks, it will come at a high probability of injury to the soft tissue of their limbs, rendering any opponentr a less effective threat. These competitive pressures challenged karate-ka from many styles and systems to delve deeper into their kata interpretations. Coincidentally, at this very point in time, historical validation of advanced grappling principles inherent in kata began to emerge. When pressed, both the Okinawans and long-term Western practitioners suddenly produced the goods. The Okinawans claimed to have had the answers all along. And real, practical, and effective kata bunkai was revealed.

How do you know Okinawan karate possesses this hidden dimension?

My most influential sensei, William Scott Russell (1946-2000) was convinced that karate training provided a supercharging of the Human Subtle Energy Body to enhance all manner of physical technique. He recognized that Isshinryu, particularly its Sanchin kata, possessed an evolutionary component within its practice (*Karate The Energy Connection,* Delacort Publishing, 1976, W.S. Russell). Russell's initial observation, in my opinion, was accurate, but it was also a gross generalization of such power potential. Nevertheless, I came to see it was near the mark of my own observations later in my career. I've searched for decades for the specifics of Russell's declaration within the Isshin kata syllabus to validate his hypothesis—with much success and continued excitement. I know today, beyond a doubt, that Isshinryu kata contain a wealth of Esoteric information on the internal nature of martial arts. Through the periodical publishing media we are occasionally given inklings of this idea with various articles hinting here and there at an internal component embedded within Isshinryu. But here we are in 2017, over sixty years from Isshinryu's introduction into the U.S., and there is still little substantial commentary on the subject for either sensei or student to sink their teeth into. We would like to bring this missing "substantial commentary" to the attention of the world's Isshinryu community and share some of our technical insights. Isshinryu and karate in general is ripe for an evolution, certainly a revolution in thinking. One must not forget, Tatsuo Shimabuku himself was a rebel. He stepped off the mainstream path of the Shorin arts to espouse what he felt were important and necessary changes. As I have commented in several articles, the best testament that I ever heard regarding an explanation for why Shimabuku created Isshinryu was the comment made by the Aikibudo expert, Arakawa Mitsugi, who stated: *"Why would a master of Shorin descent, already considered a great master, create another karate ryu almost the same as Shorin extraction but intensify its technique to a higher, more scientific tier? He did not need two arts, one in the same, but instead sought to present distinctive aspects of karate-do. Isshinryu was meant to become the hierarchy of the Shorin 'te' lines which he would elevate his black belts to study."*

Had Shimabuku lived another decade or two I do not doubt that he would have expanded his system. Tatsuo's Isshinryu lives on, not as a static entity, but as a continuously dynamic and evolving system for long term, passionate professionals like myself who simply seek more substance to our investigations. Shimabuku, like his forefathers, gave us some great building blocks from which we are still assembling ever more unique martial possibilities.

From the time of Isshinryu's creation to the time of Shimabuku's death his progenitors used this period to define the Isshinryu system. It is a valid observation to say that Tatsuo's Isshinryu was all that he taught and believed from 1956 until is death 1975. However, we in Isshin Kempo do not feel that Isshinryu simply stopped growing as a martial system, nor as a martial phenomenon in the commercial dojo world. Professionals of the Isshin arts continue Isshinryu's maturation, extending it from 1975 to the present. Speaking about our dojo alone, we have uncovered substantive technical information, which allows us to place yet another tier of informative skill sets on top of Shimabuku's already sturdy foundation.

Can you give a specific idea of what you mean by "technical evolution?"

Let's look at one specific Isshinryu trait, the thumb on top of the fist, hand formation. Isshinryu sets itself apart from many karate systems with technical distinctions like this fist formation, which is also found in the Chinese Internal art of Hsing I. Making a fist with the thumb on top of the index finger, instead of alongside it, is one of the major trademarks of the style. The common explanation given, that the thumb contracts the tendon extensors, *Pollicis Longus* and *Pollicis Brevis*, and thereby indicates a stronger fist, is *not* the rationale we accept as the central reason for this particular fist structure. Does anyone really believe that the rest of the world's martial community failed to see the fist was made stronger by placing the thumb on top of the index finger? Hardly. There is validity to the fact that the tendons are flexed with the thumb in this position, making the fist firmer, but only for pressures exerted downward on top of the fist, not pressures exerted upwards. In other words, if you are going to hammer-fist downward onto a hard object like a collarbone, placing your thumb on top of the fist will set you up for a wrist/hand injury. There is a better, more useful, reasoning beneath this common explanation that offers insight into the arts *inner* workings.

Secondly, I would like to suggest that the thumb on top of the fist was probably not, nor was it ever intended to be, an *absolute* punching action. It may have been regarded as such in Shima-buku's Isshinryu Marine Corps community, but it is not regarded as such in the Isshin Kempo system. We view the thumb on top as serving a particular, but seemingly, lost function. There are times when the thumb should be on top of the fist and times for other fist formations because the placement of the thumb acts as a piv-otal control of arm strength. In Isshin kempo we therefore present three different fist formations used respectively in the upper, mid-dle and lower target regions.

Which came first, the punch or the block?

In the 1970's I was privy to a conversation between East Coast Isshinryu master, Don Nagle and Tatsuo Shimabuku regarding the formation of the Isshinryu middle block. During Shimabuku's visit to New Jersey in 1966, he asked Sensei Nagle how he was per-forming his middle block. Nagle replied that he was doing it as taught; a three-quarter forearm block with *bent* wrist. Shimabuku told Nagle to continue to perform the technique that way while admitting that he had succumbed to pressure from the martial community to teach the forearm block *without* the bend in the wrist.

When you think *martial art*, you must think wider than a single karate technique like a punch or kick. It's important to view move-ments as packages or sets of events. Each limb configuration aug-ments, complements or contributes to one another. A punch does not exist in a vacuum without support form the rest of the body. We have stance, hip and knee placement, degrees of tension and relaxation throughout the structure, breathing considerations, nervous system reaction time, timing, etc. For example, a stance contributes to the conveyance of the force of a strike by offering a grounding resistance. It's not at all obvious how physical events are internally packaged. Many martial artists do not think about how a block *bioenergetically* supports a punch or a punch sup-ports a block, but these variables offer support in significant ways. If you execute a vertical punch right after doing a bone-edge mid-dle block, you will find that you have cut off some of the motive power for your punch. Likewise, if you throw a vertical punch after assuming an improper knee's drawn inward, Seisan stance, you will also find a reduction in punching strength. So one must as-semble techniques correctly to maximize their effects. This knowl-edge of the proper assembly of techniques is becoming a lost art, known only by a minority of the martial community. This forces the professional looking for deeper rationales to fall back on their own intuition and years of trail and error to piece this mysterious puzzle together.

The bent wrist middle block is unique because the bend allows the blocker to overlap his wrist on top of the puncher's arm. This action will affect the meridian flow to the blocker's advantage in a way a straight wrist block cannot accomplish. Maybe Shima-buku, like Funakoshi before him, recognized that students really did not want too much detail, so he decided to keep his art simple. But that doesn't help the thousands of committed Isshinryu black belts hoping to add to their own advance in the art.

Can you give an overview of Sanchin kata being practiced in the U.S. today?

When I look at the practice of Sanchin throughout the world I can make several broad and critical observations. First, I see far greater presentations of the *performance* and variety within the performances of Sanchin than the *explanations* for why the form is practiced in the manners exhibited.

The GOJU Scale

Sanchin presentations fall on what I call the *Go-Ju* spectrum. On one side we have very Hard (*Go*) versions. *Hard* refers to the degree and duration of visible physical tension held in the body via muscular contraction throughout the sequence. On the flip side we have the Soft (*Ju*) versions. Here, there is little or no visible bodily tension except for the minimal effort to hold the limbs in their proper positions. Isshinryu historically falls toward the center of this spectrum, as both a Hard and Soft form. That is, taking a cursory glance at Sanchin's outer form, we have a fairly equitable distribution of tension and relaxation occurring throughout the musculature. In a conversation with Aston Hugh, a sixty-year practitioner of martial arts and noted Isshinryu expert in the 1970's, Hugh's extensive knowledge questions the Hard style methodology of the 'Go' schools. His position is that Sanchin is a Soft form, whose mistaken heavy tension is actually the result of what is called *induced chi flow,* a phenomenon of energy build up that causes the body to contract in a specific pattern to each performer to open blocked Ki channels.

232

Why do you think there is so much variation in Sanchin performance, yet so little definition? What do you think is the purpose of the Sanchin form?

Concepts are recreated, that is, reinterpreted, every time they are passed to another person. Because of this trait we should expect to see variety in our Forms from one generation to another. Any Sanchin kata passed from a teacher to a disciple immediately becomes subject to the unique mental and physical forces residing within the recipient. Each person is exclusive by way of their body structure, perceptions, intelligence level, awareness, curiosities and cultural influences. I wouldn't expect anything less. Any astute sensei can tell you that if you take ten beginning students, teach them exactly the same Form, most will exhibit immediate nuances in their emphasis and/or pacing of the content. These distinctions will widen within three months. Likewise, pick ten sensei to perform a new kata and you will also see the same phenomenon. Consider that today's beginning students will become tomorrow's sensei. One's objectives for doing a kata can also be defined similarly. Different times, different needs, different cultural values will alter the purpose behind a kata performance. Therefore, you should not be concerned whether your kata is the absolute *correct* form, as in 'historically' correct or 'traditionally' correct, as much as trying to grasp the rationale behind doing it the way it is taught to you.

So, if your teacher tells you to do kata because its *Traditional*, or tells you it's a 'breathing' form, a 'balancing form,' or a 'fighting form,' and you can clearly see this rationale in the movement sequences, that's a good building block from which to start your study. But if you are told, *"just do it,"* without a clear explanation, this is not going to get you too far along the barefoot trail.

The other reason that we don't get much in-depth public commentary about Sanchin is that the higher end information encoded in the kata is often proprietary to the school that possesses, transmits, discovers, or develops this knowledge. It is therefore usually, or only, offered to the advanced students of that particular dojo or organization. This is an acceptable use of knowledge, as most practitioners will need to have built a firm base of understanding of their form before adding another level of skill.

There are some fundamentals however, running through most Sanchin kata. Sanchin is a multi-dimensional, multi-agenda form. It is not a fixed or single objective kata in our thinking. It might be for some teachers. For us however, Sanchin reflects a brilliant, multi-tracked purpose. Within the *chuan fa* arts, martial disciplines heavily influenced by Buddhist thought, there are three goals built into Sanchin's practice; It is practiced as a *combative* form to give us a straightforward way to deal with physical hostility. As a therapeutic form, Sanchin gives us a moving method of self-acupuncture/pressure. As a meditative vehicle, sanchin gives us both a *mantric* and *mudric* mechanism to shift consciousness by expanding our awareness in a particular manner. The terms *mantra* and *mudra*, associated more often with Indian yoga, have relevancy as well to Kata. The *mantra* refers to a type of rhythmic mindset held during kata practice. The *mudra* refers to the energetic effects the various postures and their repeated patterns have on the performers.

For the moment, I will confine my discussion of Sanchin to its value as an internal energy cultivator. This conceptual framework for the pattern runs like a continuous current from the past to the present. Let me explain this current with a simple, story-framed overview:

Let's say that a man, troubled that he will be imminently attacked, approaches a knowledgeable fighting master. This master sees that his solicitor is visibly upset, and as a consequence, physically uptight and tense. The master tells the man that his tension will work against him adding, "If you are attacked, you are going to tense. This tension will block your Ki flow. Your stiffness will deplete you of energy. So, I want you to breathe in a particular way to prevent your energy from dissipating."

The man survives his future attack, escaping with only a few bruises. Afterward, he joins the master's dojo and takes an immediate liking to *kumite*. He throws his heart into it. As months of training turn into years, he notices himself finding more and more pockets of relaxation amidst his moments of tension. His astute teacher pulls him aside. "Now that you are able to exert some control over your body in the heat of conflict, and you have learned how to relax within the fire of the fight, I am going to modify your Sanchin so that your energy moves freely.

"But what about the breathing method you taught me in the earlier version?" his student laments, having to change something he worked so hard to incorporate.

"It will no longer work under these new circumstances. You must now switch to microcosmic or/reverse breathing."

Years more go by and this once initially nervous student finds that he has mastered his craft. He can exert fine motor control over his entire body. He can stay calm through intense challenges. He has opened up his body channels and can control the flow of Ki with exceptional form.

Recognizing his disciple's skill, his teacher describes that he no longer needs to control his energy flow by means of his physical body but can be taught do so entirely through his *mental* body. "Now that you have made your physical techniques automatic, I will teach you how to adhere to the Principles—without thought." This is the threshold that separates the Form Schools from the No Form Schools.

We have different Sanchin formulas to achieve specific aims. This can be seen in the many variations of the form. For example, Isshinryu and Uechiryu Sanchin start with the opposite foot moving forward. Look closely and you may see that the hand work is also slightly different. Uechi ryu double blocks draw forward. Isshinryu's double blocks press outward. These technical nuances are often missed when trying to distinguish the proper way to perform a Sanchin.

One problem in clarifying the 'proper' Sanchin is Western culture's fixation on cognition. We seem to need, even crave, an immediate, all-defining goal for every undertaking, even to take a single step. It's as if you can't ride your bike unless you know where you are going! I had a young student once ask, "Why should I learn kata? And a more advance student ask, "What is the difference between my own made up kata and these 'old' forms?" For all its simplicity in looks, Sanchin is a complex form.

Sensei can degrade kata when they explain them too broadly or squeeze them into a narrow focus, such as labeling Sanchin *solely* as a breathing form, a tension form, a fighting form etc. Sanchin is all of the above and more. I find that most discussions about Sanchin quickly drift either into ambiguity, or egocentric debate once you go past the breathing, fighting, tension aspects. Too often the definition of Sanchin starts from vagueness and ends in vagueness.

Sanchin's purpose, as the name indicates, 'triple-layer conflict' or 'three battles,' despite some of the popular literature denying this value, was designed as a whole person exercise to explore and evaluate the interrelationships between one's physical, mental/emotional and energetic dimensions. The overarching goal is to broaden us as humans.

For me the central question is, 'why *this* particular format, this particular pattern? Why can't Seisan or Seiuchin kata guide me through these *three battles of existence* with the same value?' To a lesser extent, they can. But Sanchin was created for this very purpose and is therefore a better vehicle for this undertaking.

I initially hit a big wall trying to answer the question, "Why is Sanchin kata the best sequence for this venture with so many variations in existence? Do I start with a Chinese *Sam Chien* variant, a Uechi or Goju variation? Or do I look to the foundational forms or styles, like White Crane that Sanchin evolved from? Do all Sanchin's reach the same goal or do they take us to different endpoints? Where does one even begin with this line of questioning?

I eventually chose my course. I would start with the fundamentals of physical motion. I asked the most basic of questions about physical movement in search of deeper rationales. For example, why does the Isshinryu Sanchin kata start by stepping with the right foot forward into Sanchin dachi? Why not a left foot forward, like the Uechi version? Why does Shimabuku bend his elbows on the spear/presses while other variations have a slightly, or radically different motion? Why did Chojun Miyagi close the hands into fists when the Chinese Shaolin versions kept the hands open? Why did Miyagi add the second Dharma Wheel circle at the end of the kata? To get to the bottom of these questions I had to fall back on a better understanding of the effects of the most basic movements on physical strength. Why do humans move at all in the manner that we do? My simple inquiry had far-reaching consequences.

If you take the position that all the kata moves have specific bunkai and this is what lights up or activates a kata, what are those bunkai? Are they fixed, fluid or tiered? How were they determined? Wouldn't it make more sense that such bunkai would be firmly stapled onto the kata? Why aren't the Sanchin's of the world all being taught with clearly presented bunkai or explanation? A few minutes on Youtube will show you that they are not. And yes, I take a strong position that Sanchin has practical application value.

You have spent the last twenty-five years of a lengthy forty-five year teaching career investigating the Internal aspects of Isshinryu. Why is it so important that martial artists studying Isshinryu be exposed to this level of training?

I wrote this book for two reasons. The Eosteric Teachings are a disappearing art in Asia. They may be lost altogether. Mainstream Isshinryu practitioners are not aware that profound internal aspects reside within their art, so they are not looking in this direction of study. If someone doesn't attempt a revival of the Esoteric Teachings here in the West, such perspectives could be lost forever or only ever known by small, dedicated groups. Secondly, I think life is best enjoyed when it's shared with others. I share my knowledge of the hidden dimensions of Isshinryu with my senior students and all interested parties. Because this subject has proven equally stimulating and meaningful to my students, it makes my research all the more worthwhile. I am sure many of the ancient masters realized that whatever knowledge they held as they reached advanced ages could never be passed fully to a novice. There just wouldn't be enough time. If a student arrived at my door today to learn all that I have gained, I could teach that student for twenty years. Will I be around that long?

How did you arrive at all the insights that you have presented in this work?

I am a career student and teacher of Okinawan karate-dō. I teach and practice karate as a way of life, not just as a physical, self-defense system. I am a Buddhist monk in the Chen Yen Shingon Mikkyo sect, once a bodyguard art that used martial arts as a means to self-discovery and personal evolution. Most of my insights for this book come from nearly five decades of direct knowledge and study along with access to vital Esoteric Teachings. Confirmation and validation of the theories I've presented also comes from twenty-five years of testing and research with the collaboration of a core of dedicated, advanced students and outside experts, many with ten to sixty years experience in this and other martial disciplines.

CONCLUSION

There is no technical ceiling to Okinawan Isshinryu except that which an organization, sensei, or student choses to put into place.

Isshinryu continues to exert its influence. The more open dialogs and stories we can generate about the full face of the Isshin arts, the better sense we will all have of its future direction and success.

THE GREATEST REBEL OF ALL

On January 15, 1954 on the tiny Japanese island in the town of Navo, a forty-eight year old, talented Shorin ryu karate master, named Tatsuo Shimabuku, broke from his martial traditions to take a bold new stance. He created a radically new martial system, Isshinryu, 'the undivided method'. On that same day, having made his decision to break from tradition he joined the ranks of an elite cadre of individuals. He became a rebel, a maverick. Like any true rebel, when tradition limits them, they buck its rigidity, shed the conventional, and hack a new path into the dense jungle of the unknown. Shimabuku did what all true rebels do. He listened to the beat of his own heart.

In taking this gamble Shimabuku paid the price of all rebels. By severing his roots, he lost disciples and favor amongst some of the elite martial art organizations. He met resistance. But rebel Shimabuku was a fighter. Rebellious fighters don't give ground easily. By choosing to do things his way he won a personal victory over himself and stimulated thousands of students worldwide who followed his style and methods of teaching to the present day. Shimabuku persevered until the age of 66. He died on May 30, 1975. I believe Shimabuku found his reward in his martial art, his one heart's love. Since his death the spirit of his martial pulse throbs in bodies and minds of thousands of Isshinryu practitioners around the world. I was one of those bitten by the art of Isshinryu. Who could have guessed his seed would have sprouted so many ardent disciples and changed the course of my own life.

Shimabuku passed away when I was twenty-five years old. Though he visited the States several times, I never met him. By the time of his death I had been in karate nine years. Five of which I taught full time. I was a young and mostly naive instructor for a large and successful karate school in Summit, New Jersey, that would become one of the State's pioneering dojos. Though I regret not meeting Shimabuku, in a strange way, I feel that I have shared something of his struggles in the martial arts. It could be said the mind of a karate master lives on in his kata. I've inhabited Shimabuku's kata my entire adulthood. I have carried the baton of Isshinryu handed to me as a young man, steadfastly to the age of sixty-six as of this writing. I have taught the Isshinryu art for forty-six years to thousands of students. I have devoted my entire adult life in the pursuit of martial knowledge. Proudly, I have witnessed my own seeds grow into many, firm trees.

Once a man has gathered the necessary life tools for his survival, he does not need any justification walking his own path. It simply becomes a question of courage and honesty to walk it tall to the end. A rebel's journey is particularly difficult because it goes against the general current. It's also personal. It may draw suspect glances and asides from the political right if you don't walk with the same stride, with the same button down conventionality as the Establishment. When you turn off the main thoroughfare to seek your unique path, your only guide will be your inner voice and your convictions. Resistance, resentment, doubt, confusion and ridicule may become your fiercest opponents hurled at you from all sides, inside and out. Resistance may emerge far afield of your habitat or spring from the most intimate corners of your dojo. One needs a strong vision to trek off the beaten trail.

In my opinion, we are all rebels when it comes to the fight to understand the meaning and realities of our own lives. We have only ourselves to rely upon in today's often tribeless and unsupportive communities. How you train, how you assess your opponent's strengths and weaknesses, how effectively you apply your wisdom, will determine your success or failure in the many arenas you will find yourselves.

In naming his style, I do not know if Shimabuku meant that 'one heart' was needed to make the journey, or that 'one heart' would be found along the way. I don't think it matters. They are both valid quests. I do know that the 'heart' represents the essential core of one's being, the *Kensho* experience, where one's conviction is

239

tempered in the heat of passion. Shimabuku's one heart method offered me a way to connect with my core self.

At seventeen years old I saw Isshinryu as a lethal weapon, practical and efficient. I pursued that end to crush and check my personal fears, even though I rarely encountered any outside adversaries. I have since learned that Isshinryu runs a deeper course. I now see it as a vital Life tool. We have too many weapons of destruction in this world and too few instruments to rebuild or recreate a nourishing life. I suppose this is the fulcrum in thinking that once opened a path from the *jutsu* (technique) into the *Do* (Way). The quality that makes one person spiritual and the other material is *attitude*, a change and a choice in perspective. When you stop viewing your art as a weapon for your injured or arrogant ego, and instead see it for its potential as a spiritual tool, your art will transition to a higher road. Digging for the best treasures of self, for the greatest wisdom, for the sharpest skills, is the goal of my martial art. You will find buoyant treasure on the surface, but only in the fathoms of the mind and body will you find the richest reward. Isshinryu has become one of my surest Life steppingstones. It has allowed me to excavate my authentic self.

The greatest rebel I have ever encountered has been the Rebel Isshinryu, the art that has taught me how to intelligently and effectively engage my adversaries in every arena they should appear, however diverse or unexpected, and even if I find that I am the fiercest enemy of all. For some of you, your opponents may not at all be what you expect. The most difficult will be your own mind.

In this book I have shared with you what I know of this Rebel discipline. It is not the Isshinryu of Tatsuo Shimabuku. That was his personal tool and stamp on his art. The spirit of Isshinryu is tied to my path. This is the Isshinryu that will lead to the victory over oneself. For each of us must temper Isshinryu in the fire of our own sweat in the grand Dojo of Life.

REBEL ISSHINRYU's
Graphic Elements

CHALLENGE 1 – Isshinryu's thumb-on-top fist formation is one of the most distinguishing characteristics of the style and distinctly different from both mainstream Western and Eastern fists.

CHALLENGE 2 – Like a calligraphy brush stroke on a blank canvas, one's *kihon* (basics) represent the seeds of an ever-unfolding complexity.

CHALLENGE 3 – All actions fall within the transformative processes portrayed by one of China's oldest symbols, the Bagua (8 Diagrams). The Bagua, like the binary code forming the image of the kicker, provides us with a template for understanding the higher end principles of Energy (Kiko) work.

CHALLENGE 4 – A young boy performs in front of a panel of judges during a New Jersey, Garden State Games tournament from the book, *The Wind Warrior: Training of A Karate Champion*, Goedecke, 1992.

CHALLENGE 5 – A Youtube video clip captures Tatsuo Shimabuku performing a hook block from the Seiuchin kata on one his visits to the United States.

CHALLENGE 6 – Former Isshin Kempo Sensei, Joe Noonan, gives a martial talk. A spherical Yin/Yang is superimposed to convey the need for instructors to help students understand complex training concepts.

CHALLENGE 7 – Energy moving thru precise pathways in the body gave rise to the movement patterns we call *kata*. The Sanchin performer is shown with a diagram of Ki flow over his dantien, the area around the navel, considered the seat of physical power.

CHALLENGE 8 – A series of crescent steps form a distinct pattern in the sand.

CHALLENGE 9 – Shifu Hayashi demonstrates the technical subtleties between the Kiba and Seiuchin stances.

CHALLENGE 10 – The *rei* (bow), like the delicate flowers that border Hayashi, contains many hidden nuances both martial and social.

CHALLENGE 11 – Rokudan (6th dan), Tim Smith mimics a samurai's sword posture using a *hanbo* (short staff) instead of a sword. Clothing contributes subtle energy to the swordsman that a T-shirt and gi pants do not. Steel versus wood weapons also have very different energy signatures.

CHALLENGE 12 – A Kiai at a specific tonal frequency will disrupt the physical strength of the opponent.

CHALLENGE 13 – A photo overlay captures Hayashi performing the *Neko Dachi* (Cat stance) simultaneously in two directions on top of Mount Daniel, British Columbia, 2007.

CHALLENGE 14 – Of the two primary forearm blocks taught by Shimabuku, the topmost became the preferred method.

CHALLENGE 15 – A multi-armed Hindu diety, flanked with mirror images of Hayashi doing high blocks, suggests that simple blocking actions offer more than one interpretation.

CHALLENGE 16 – These three punches represent the majority of the world's primary punching fist postures.

CHALLENGE 17 – Two feet standing in front of the outline of a battery highlight the electro-magnetic properties of the left and right legs.

CHALLENGE 18 – Like bullets in a pistol's chamber, fist are often primed at the sides of the body just before a Traditional punching drill.

CHALLENGE 19 – The label for some technique creates an illusion that punches can only be punches, blocks can only be blocks, kicks must only be kicks. Hayashi demonstrates a high block attack to the neck of his opponent.

CHALLENGE 20 – After intercepting a punch, Hayashi inserts a rising spear hand between the arm and torso of his partner to set up for a joint lock maneuver.

CHALLENGE 21 – Pressure on the head of an acupuncture model suggests that pressure point work is neither simple nor always easy to activate.

CHALLENGE 22 – This is part of an original painting by Shifu Hayashi of a Nio Guardian (benevolent king), protector of the Dharma, hinting at a deeper essence and goal behind our training—to achieve enlightenment.

CHALLENGE 23 – Each kata in Isshinryu's syllabus can be represented as one spoke in the stone carving of the Buddhist Dharma Wheel. Sanchin can be considered the hub or center supplying each of the remaining fighting forms with vital Energy principles.

CHALLENGE 24 – Hayashi corrects the form of young Nick Armitage, today an advanced Isshin Kempo sensei and career Grand Teton National Park Ranger. The image comes from the Book, *The Wind Warrior, Training of a Karate Champion.* Goedecke/Hausherr, 1992

CHALLENGE 25 – Hayashi demonstrates a double wrist and shoulder lock found in the opening moves of Seisan kata. This is just one of Isshinryu's many standing submission sequences.

CHALLENGE 26 – The purity of a kata, like the purity of a premium Chinese tea, along with the skill of the tea server, makes all the difference in conveying the essence of our fighting forms.

CHALLENGE 27 – An advanced adult class demonstrates the opening section of the Seiuchin kata.

CHALLENGE 28 – No one is trying to become a Shimabuku clone. To be a truly autonomous martial artist each person must find his own style within the style.

CHALLENGE 29 – Carved figurines of a rabbit and turtle convey the changing cadence of a kata. The wooden sculpture of the old man carrying two buckets of water suggests we weigh the value of our rhythmic movements through life.

CHALLENGE 30 – A heel kick can be a devastating front kick maneuver while protecting the small bones of the foot and toes.

CHALLENGE 31 – Just as nature's winds can shape a tree, proper breathing can shape the power of a karate technique as well as the long-term health and vitality of the disciple.

CHALLENGE 32 – A left foot, lead cat stance is a superior energy-drawing posture when coupled with a soft, lead open hand and proper breathing.

CHALLENGE 33 – Senior Isshin Kempo rokudan (6th dan), Tian Zhua, demonstrates a *Ju* version of the Dharma Wheel circles that end the Sanchin kata.

CHALLENGE 34 – A single sai is displayed, the weapon of choice used in civil defense during the Ming dynasty in China. Unarmed practice of the sai may be the reason some empty-hand kata were not initially well understood in Okinawa.

CHALLENGE 35 – A student ponders the Isshinryu code's enigmatic meaning. Holistic study embraces the physical, mental and spiritual dimensions of training. Non-physical martial training, like reading, viewing or discussing the art, is considered 'soft' training.

CHALLENGE 36 – The left leg is depicted with a fist replacing the foot, suggesting that 'fisting' the toes in Sanchin stance can actually lead to the opposite results.

CHALLENGE 37 – The *Sri Yantra* is one of India's most ancient and sacred symbols. Here it is superimposed over an Isshinryu Siesan kata move. The Esoteric Teachings use complex symbolism to convey the intricate interplay of both cosmic and earthly influences on man.

CHALLENGE 38 – Leaves and martial artists are randomly blown about in the air. Some students may feel adrift, trying to find grounding in their kata training. Why this move and not that one? Why this kata and not another?

CHALLENGE 39 – A student standing near a banana peel suggests that it is not uncommon for one to slip up on unfamiliar concepts buried within simple technique.

CHALLENGE 40 – Hayashi's black obi, awarded in 1971, is wrapped around a bronze art sculpture of a Dharma wheel. The '*Om Mani Padme Hum*' mantra (chant) is carved into the cylinder.

CHALLENGE 41 – A happy young Karate girl wears the entire belt rank sequence of Isshin Kempo. Our martial evolution is captured in the ascending colored belt-ranking system.

CHALLENGE 42 – The elector-magnetic currents of a dipole are superimposed over a karate gi. Even inanimate objects can affect one's physical strength.

CHALLENGE 43 – The young man on the left tests for his shodan grade in a match with a senior black belt. As part of his test he must fight all the senior students of his school.

CHALLENGE 44 – The Tori gate is a symbolic marker of the transition from the profane to the sacred, from the empirical to the spiritual.

CHALLENGE 45 – A diagram of Ki flow is overlaid on the bodies of two thirty-year kata experts. The arrows hint at the intricate internal manipulations that can create exceptionally strong technique, something a video cannot convey.

CHALLENGE 46 – A Feng Shui Compass, a device used to determine the energetic influences within a defined space, is superimposed over the dojo during an adult karate class in the 1980's. One's dojo environment can be greatly enhanced by adhering to Feng Shui principles.

CHALLENGE 47 – The kanji for the word Ki appears as a steam floating above a bowl of rice. This kanji is precisely what the pictograph of 'Ki' literally means.

CHALLENGE 48 – Many martial artists move blindly through their kata unable to see its full depth of knowledge.

CHALLENGE 49 – Although the modern expectation is to find everything one needs to know on the Internet, many martial mysteries still challenge us and remain to be explored.

CHALLENGE 50 – A shovel and a hand-made wooden treasure box in the dirt suggest that future treasures are to be unearthed if one is willing to dig deeper into their art.

CHALLENGE 51 – Isshin Kempo teacher Tom Maloney demonstrates that, over time, like the sands of the hourglass, the true nature of a martial art is to balance oneself in all aspects of one's existence. After the practical concerns are achieved, the martial adept will begin the larger quest to balance one's overall life energy, similar to the aims of the yogis of India.

CHALLENGE 52 – A Buddhist, right-facing *Svastika* forms the basic embusen (floor symbol) for an I Form pattern once taught by Shimabuku. The compass embedded in the center of the Svastika highlights the role directionality plays in effective kata activation.

CHALLENGE 53 – Hayashi clasps a brass *dorje* or *vajra*, the Thunderbolt, used as a weapon and symbol of the thunderous power inherent in the Buddhist teachings. Buddhist influence runs throughout the Isshinryu kata. Shimabuku was a Buddhist.

CHALLENGE 54 – An Isshin Kempo shodan performs a move from the Neihanchi kata while facing a brick wall. The photo suggests that sometimes one may find him or herself up against a brick wall when trying to figure out why a kata was constructed in a particular manner.

CHALLENGE 55 – A feather sitting atop a stone suggests that Sanchin is neither a completely hard nor soft practice. Sanchin kata performances can cover a wide range of expressions referred to as the *Goju* (Hard/Soft) scale.

CHALLENGE 56 – Shifu Hayashi is captured in a photo as a young man in his 20's in the mid-1970's, doing a move from Sunsu kata at the Livingston, NJ branch of the Isshin Kempo Association where he served as a senior instructor for one of the State's largest dojos.

CHALLENGE 57 – Two karateka depicted as martial doctors contemplate both the depth and future of Isshinryu system as their vehicle for advancement.

BOOKS BY HAYASHI TOMIO
(Christopher J. Goedecke)

Internal Karate: Mind Matters and the
Seven Gates of Power

The Soul Polisher's Apprentice: A Martial Kumite
About Personal Evolution

Wind Warrior: Training Of A Karate Champion

Smart Moves: A Kid's Guide to Self Defense

The Unbreakable Board & The Red Dragon Surprise

Interested in a seminar on the Esoteric Teachings?

Contact:

Shifu Hayashi Tomio
windschool@earthlink.net

Read or listen to Shifu's works at
isshinkempo.com

Made in the USA
Monee, IL
03 September 2021

77315206R00134